TEACHING LANGUAGE-DISABLED CHILDREN

A COMMUNICATION GAMES INTERVENTION

Susan Conant,
Milton Budoff,
and
Barbara Hecht

BROOKLINE
BOOKS
Cambridge, MA

Library of Congress Cataloging in Publication Data

Conant, Susan J., 1946–
   Teaching language-disabled children.

   Bibliography: p.
   1. Language disorders in children. 2. Educational games. I. Budoff, Milton, 1929– . II. Hecht, Barbara, 1953– . III. Title.
RJ496.L35C66 1983   371.91′4   83-27303
ISBN 0-914797-38-7
ISBN 0-914797-04-2 (pbk.)

Published by
Brookline Books
PO Box 1046
Cambridge, MA 02238

Printed in the United States of America

To Jessica

PREFACE

While teachers and speech therapists are frequently urged to help children use language plentifully, appropriately, and effectively in day-to-day interactions with adults and peers, recommendations about how to provide this help are often vague. Recommendations are often for activities that occur in any competent teacher's classroom or for activities in which children produce utterances without conveying meaning.

The purpose of this book is to provide a detailed description of the communication games. The series of games described provides a specific yet conversational way to help children learn to use language. The games are simple, noncompetitive, structured activities. This book describes exactly how to play the communication games; it does not simply exhort practitioners to give topic-relevant responses and to take advantages of opportunities for communication. The games create those opportunities. This approach involves specific teaching methods and not simply a new perspective on language remediation. Finally, this method is communicative in ways that traditional methods are not; in playing the games, children use words to convey meaning and do not pointlessly produce utterances.

Contents

Chapter 1 describes the communicative method used in the games and contrasts it with traditional methods. The chapter includes a description of the basic structure of communication games and the steps followed in playing them. Chapter 2 provides guidelines for assessing the appropriateness of children for this program. Chapter 3 describes the program levels and the process of matching children and games — which games to play with which children. Chapter 4 discusses options for working with children (arrangements of players) and the interpersonal implications of the arrangements.

Chapters 5 through 10 are concerned with different game formats. Chapters 11 and 12 explain the linguistic content that the games can teach and the design and construction of games to teach that content. Chapter 13 is a brief description of how to conduct a language intervention session using the games, while chapter 14 discusses tactics for using the games effectively and common impediments to the transition from traditional to communicative language teaching. Readers who are interested only in the instructions for playing the games, including those who prefer to learn the approach by trying it, should skim chapter 1, then read chapters 5 through 10.

Terminology

Academic disciplines concerned with language employ many technical terms. They also provide a variety of definitions for terms whose meanings most speakers take for granted. For example, *communication*, *information*, and *meaning* are loaded words for students of language. What kinds of communication? Whose meaning? In what sense informative?

In this book, technical terms have been avoided whenever ordinary language provides simple equivalents. Consequently, we have used some words in ways that will strike linguists and language philosophers as unforgivably rough or loose. This book, however, is for practitioners, not linguists and language philosophers. For instance, *achieve definite reference* is avoided when *mean* does just as well. Thus, the linguist or philosopher who comes across rough uses of delicate words is warned in advance. In particular, our use of the word *communicate* usually means to achieve definite reference or to spell out propositional information.

Development

The games described in this book were developed in three phases. The first phase took place during Barbara Hecht and Robert Morse's work with mentally retarded and language-delayed children in several public-school classrooms. The second and third phases took place in a project supported by Grant #G007904630 from the Office of Special Education, United States Department of Education.

During the second phase, project staff provided direct service to 40 young, language-disabled children two or three times each week. The children were an extremely heterogeneous group in terms of etiology and diagnosis. The group included children with Down's syndrome, cultural-familial mental retardation, minimal brain damage, developmental delays, aphasia, autistic-like symptoms, unexplained language delays, and other diagnoses. All of these children had very serious language disabilities. Most were chronically silent in their classrooms; when they did speak, they said very little. Often, what they said was very difficult to understand because of articulation or voice disorders. The games were, in short, developed mainly during intensive work with a highly varied group of seriously handicapped children. In addition, the disabled and nondisabled classmates of these children frequently participated in the games. During the second year of this phase, we also worked in public-school classrooms with special-needs children and in classrooms located in a community mental health and mental retardation center.

In the third phase, speech and language pathologists, teachers, and assistant teachers used the games and contributed many new ones. They provided us with feedback about games and about our efforts to describe games and playing strategies. While many of their specific contributions are noted in the text, their influence is considerably more pervasive than the specific notes would suggest.

ACKNOWLEDGEMENTS

We would particularly like to thank the following practitioners for their participation in the development of this program and for generously welcoming us into their programs: Gary Bechtold, Jean Berolzheimer, Donna Cavanaugh, Ann Englund, Ann Hardiman, Mary Harrington, Kathy Hawes, Zovig Kanarian, Mary Kelly, Kathy Lockyer, Sue Morris, Laurie Nee, Marsha Seletsky, Susan Shaw, Ann Whaley Tobin, Jessica Weissman, Cindy Wilson, Eleanore Lewis, Sandy Black, Judith Medalia, Catherine Marchant, and James Earley. We also want to thank Marsha Morgan and Patrick O'Neill for their preparation of the manuscript. Many able students and research assistants also contributed, especially Debby Abelman, Emily Cahan, Donna Leger, and Debbie Tolman.

Most importantly, we want to thank Cathleen Cuneo, the field coordinator of the project, for her help throughout. Her creativity, talent, and perceptiveness have been invaluable. Many of the descriptions in this book of the way the ideal clinician works are, in fact, descriptions of the way Cathy works.

Susan Conant
Milton Budoff
Barbara Hecht

Table of Contents

1

Communicative Means for Communicative Ends

When introducing the communication games to teachers and speech therapists, we are usually asked to explain how this program differs from "what we're already doing." This program differs from most other language and speech activities in method more than in aim. Teachers and speech therapists aim at helping children use language effectively and appropriately in a wide variety of contexts; their aim is to facilitate the development of communication skills; their aim, then, is communicative. The method described in this book differs from other methods in the use of communicative means to fulfill that aim.

Communicative and Noncommunicative Methods

The difference between communicative and noncommunicative methods of language teaching is evident in the following example: A teacher wants to help children use words to request juice during snack time. The teacher knows that the children want and expect the juice. The children know that the teacher has a supply of juice. In an effort to inject a need to talk into this

3

situation, teachers frequently have the children ask for juice before it is given to them. If the child wants the juice, he or she is required to use words. Sometimes the child must say *juice*, and sometimes the child must use a full sentence, such as *I want juice*. Although the aim here is to help the child use language communicatively, the child's production of *I want juice* is, in this context, noninformative. The child does not tell the teacher anything that the teacher does not already know.

Consider a second example: A teacher provides two pitchers of juice at snack time, one of apple juice and the other of orange juice. The teacher gives cups to the children and holds the two pitchers of juice. The teacher then asks: "What kind of juice do you want, apple juice or orange juice?". In this situation, the children have information to communicate that the teacher does not already have—namely, their choice of juice. The child who says *apple juice* uses words to make a specific request. In this example, the teacher's method and aim are communicative.

In the first example, the teacher did not give the child juice unless the child asked. In the second example, the teacher did not know what kind of juice to give unless the child communicated a choice.

Two examples from a formal, structured teaching situation also illustrate the difference between communicative and noncommunicative methods. In the first example, a teacher is playing Lotto with a child. To make Lotto a game involving words, the teacher institutes the following rule: When the teacher holds up a picture card, the child is permitted to claim the card if and only if the child correctly names the picture shown on the card. If the teacher holds up a picture of a cat, the child may claim the picture only by saying *cat* or *I have the cat*. The child's utterance does not tell the teacher anything new; the teacher already knows that the picture shows a cat.

In the second example, the need to use words is created in a different way. Instead of displaying the picture, the teacher deliberately conceals the picture while describing it (*I have a cat. Does anyone have a cat?*). The teacher and child reverse roles so that the child is the speaker in the game. The child then needs to say "cat" or ask "Who has the cat?" to tell the teacher which card is being used. This game is structured so that information is not equally available to the participants. The participants need to talk in order to play.

Noncommunicative methods are characterized by arbitrary demands to talk. If the child does not talk, then the teacher refuses to do something. In contrast, communicative methods create a genuine need for talk. If the child does not talk, then the adult does not know what to do. In the noncommunicative examples, the child does not do anything with words except comply with an arbitrary demand. In the communicative examples, the child does something. The child who says "apple juice" selects something. The child who says "cat" tells the teacher which card is being played.

Several other features generally distinguish traditional from communicative methods. In traditional methods, the child is often asked to repeat model sounds, words, phrases, or sentences spoken by the adult. In communicative methods, exact repetition of an adult's model phrase is pointless. What matters is the communicative adequacy of the child's message, not the particular form the child uses. The message gets across whether the child says "apple juice" or "apple" or "I want apple juice" or "'Gimme' apple." The adult may offer a model for the child to use in talking (*You want apple? Apple juice?*), but the adult does not insist that the child repeat, nor does the adult insist on any one predetermined means of asking for something.

There are two specific kinds of arbitrary demands frequently evident in noncommunicative language activities: a demand for articulatory clarity unrelated to meaning and a demand for fully formed sentences when phrases are communicatively adequate. When a child says "'duce,'" the teacher may insist that the child try to approximate *juice*. Similarly, the adult may insist that the child say *I want juice* even when *juice* alone conveys meaning equally well. The latter demand is particularly notable in the efforts of teachers and speech therapists to have children name pictures by saying "This is a cat" rather than by using nouns alone.

In the communication games described in this book, there is no demand for articulatory clarity or for particular constructions except when they are necessary to convey meaning; the purpose of games is to make them necessary. If a child pronounces a word so unclearly that the listener cannot understand it, then there is a genuine need for the child to improve articulation. If a child produces one word when the listener needs two pieces of information, then there is a genuine need for a grammatical construction.

Rewards

In many behavior-modification programs, children are given rewards for talking that bear no relationship to the content of what the child said. A child may, for example, be given M & M's as a reward for any and all utterances that meet with the trainer's approval. A somewhat looser form of behavior modification frequently observed in classrooms is the teacher's use of the phrase "Good talking!" as positive social reinforcement. For instance, the child may exclaim: "Billy blowing big bubbles!". Instead of responding to the content of the child's message, the teacher responds to the form by saying: "Good talking!".

The assumption implicit in this reinforcement is that responses related to meaning are not effective positive reinforcements. This is an assumption of questionable validity. The main problem created by interjections of *Good talking!* is not its value as a reinforcer but the effect of this kind of adult utterance on the flow of conversation. *Good talking!* introduces an abrupt shift in the topic of conversation. If the teacher provides social reinforcement related to meaning (e.g., "Yes, aren't they big bubbles!"), then the child is primed to continue to converse about the same topic. *Good talking!* is a hard speech act to follow.

In addition to providing the child with positive reinforcement, the use of *Good talking!* is intended to direct the child's attention to his or her own speech. The assumption seems to be that heightened conscious awareness facilitates the acquisition of language. The effect of awareness on different aspects of language use is unknown. It is clear, however, that children first acquiring their native language do not receive "*Good talking!* kinds of comments" from adults and are unaware of their own and others' language until long after they have begun to comprehend and produce language in rather complicated ways. The awareness of language lags far behind its use. As Cazden (1972) writes, for example: "When they're five to six years old, children recapitulate at the metalinguistic level of conscious awareness the development from telegraphic to complete sentences that they went through when they were two to three years old at the linguistic level of nonconscious oral speech." (p. 86-87) While conscious awareness seems to facilitate the development of certain sophisticated aspects of language use, it seems not to be a mechanism of young children's initial language acquisition. Furthermore, when parents provide reinforcement for talking, they expand and extend children's utterances, contribute information of interest, and otherwise pay attention to content but not to form (Brown & Hanlon, 1970; Cazden, 1972; Cook-Gumperz, 1979). *Good talking!*, then, far from helping children to improve their language use, seems likely to direct their attention away from factors that seem to be mechanisms in language acquisition (e.g., having some content to convey) and toward factors that are involved in sophisticated aspects of language use but are probably not involved in initial language acquisition.

The adult utterance of *Good talking!* also contributes to a definition of the roles of the adult and child that hinders the development of the roles of conversants or coparticipants. Grice (1975) describes the "cooperative principle" involved in conversational contributions as follows: "Make your conversational contribution such as is required at the stage at which it occurs, by the accepted purpose or direction of the talk exchange in which you are engaged." (p. 45). This principle has several attendant maxims that may be summarized as follows: Be as informative as required but no more so; do not say what you believe to be false or that for which you lack evidence; be relevant; avoid obscurity and ambiguity; be brief and orderly. The adult utterance of *Good talking!* following a child's exclamation, question, or statement violates several of these maxims. The adult is not informative in saying nothing about what the child has said. The adult's remark is irrelevant to the content of the child's utterance. Finally, the adult's remark is probably obscure and unclear to the child. What does good talking have to do with bubbles?

These violations of the cooperative principle are important because conversation seems to be the most effective language development activity yet discovered (Cook-Gumperz, 1979). To violate the cooperative principle is to destroy the interpersonal situation that seems to be most facilitative of language acquisition.

The adult who responds to a child's utterance by indicating comprehension, interest, and pleasure provides powerful positive reinforcement that does not have the many disadvantages of *Good talking!* The adult then primes the child to continue the conversation, maintains the role of coparticipant in conversation, and otherwise contributes to the continuation rather than to the termination of verbal interchanges about the child's chosen conversational topic.

In the communication games, considerable reward is provided for talking. The child who succeeds in conveying a message receives the reward of having communicated effectively. The game works in some way — pictures match toys, pictures match each other, a hidden object is revealed, or something else happens — in which the adult and other children understand their next moves. Furthermore, the adult shows obvious delight in the children's speech production by smiling, hugging, cuddling, laughing, and responding with relevant conversational contributions. The adult wants to hear the child continue to talk and provides responses that encourage the child to say more about the topic of conversation. In short, the games concentrate and heighten the rewarding features of natural conversation.

Corrections

As Brown and Hanlon (1970) discuss, parents seem to correct children on the basis of the truth value of statements, not on the basis of grammar. In the communication games, adults point out miscommunications, but they do not draw children's attention to features of talk unrelated to meaning.

The issue of correcting children is particularly evident when teachers and therapists correct children's misarticulations and telegraphic speech. In correcting articulation and in demanding long utterances, teachers are seldom in a position to give any solid reasons for not accepting the children's initial utterances. Because the child who says "'tuck'" for *truck* is clear and communicative, and because teachers sensibly want to avoid negatively reinforcing the child's talk, teachers usually issue corrections in a highly attentuated manner. Fortunately, one does not hear teachers say "Bad talking!". On the other hand, one seldom hears clear feedback about miscommunications.

In playing the communication games, adults provide feedback about the child's effectiveness and ineffectiveness in conveying referential information. Because, however, the child and adult focus on the content of messages, feedback about miscommunication is not global feedback about the child. A few examples illustrate this point.

Many language-disabled children have relatively severe articulation disorders. In the communication games, the child who says "'tuck'" for *truck* and who otherwise misarticulates in a way unrelated to meaning is not corrected in any way. As discussed in this book, there are ways to create a need for specific kinds of articulatory clarity — for instance, in games in which *pie*, *pipe*, *drum*, *thumb*, and other such pairs are involved. Communicating anything verbally requires some clarity of articulation. The communicative approach, then, does not ignore articulation. When particular misarticulations or general problems of articulation, volume, and pitch interfere with the listener's comprehension, the listener provides feedback. The adult may say, for instance: "I can't hear you" or "I can't understand. Tell me again." The adult provides clear information about the ineffectiveness of the child's effort to communicate and simultaneously provides a genuine reason for the child to improve articulation. Weiner and Ostrowski (1979) report that feedback to the effect that adults were uncertain about what children had said was effective in helping preschoolers to improve their articulation. In that study, the investigators pretended to be uncertain. In the communication games, there is no need for pretense. If one is playing a Lotto Game with a child who does not show a card but describes it incomprehensibly, one genuinely needs to request clarification. If a child speaks too softly to be heard, sticks his fingers in his mouth and mumbles, or otherwise talks unclearly, one's incomprehension is a good reason to insist upon clarity.

These same processes occur when multiword utterances are elicited. The child who says "truck" is often asked to say "This is a truck" or "I want the truck" or otherwise provide a full sentence, however superfluous the words other than *truck* may be in the speech act the child intends to perform. In the communication games, superfluous elements are treated as such. If *truck* works within the context of a game, there is no good reason to ask the child to say anything else.

The Playing Process

The communication games range in difficulty from simple games suitable for children who produce only a few words to challenging games for children who produce multiword utterances. The games use a variety of formats and teach a variety of linguistic content. While the level of difficulty, the format, and the content may differ, the basic structure of the playing process is the same in all games.

Roles

In every game the participants share two roles: those of "speaker" and "listener." The speaker has information unavailable to the listener that the listener needs to play the game. The listener, fulfilling a complementary role, needs the information the speaker has. The roles of speaker and listener may be shared by more than two players. For example, one player may be the speaker while two or three players are the listeners.

Rules

All of the games have only one basic rule: Use words. The speaker must communicate the needed information to the listener by talking.

Turns

The players take turns playing the roles of speaker and listener. The child first learning to play a game begins in the role of listener. The players then reverse roles and do so continuously as the game goes on. "Speaker" does not mean "teacher."

Process

The process of playing any of the communication games takes place in five steps.

The first step, a check on prerequisite skills, occurs only at the beginning of a game a child has not played before. The adult checks to make sure that the child has the picture recognition, matching, or other skills a game requires. In the second step, one player, whom we shall call Player A, takes the role of speaker; the other player, Player B, is the listener. Player A conveys information previously unavailable to Player B, and Player B makes a move in the game on the basis of that information. In the third step, the players evaluate the effectiveness of the communication: Did the message get across? Fourth, the players exchange roles. Player A is the listener, and Player B is the speaker. Player B now has information unavailable to Player A and conveys that information. Player A makes a move in the game on the basis of Player B's message. Fifth, the players again evaluate the effectiveness of the communication. The players then reverse roles, and the process begins again at the second step.

When a child is first learning a game format, Player A is an adult; the adult models the production of messages before the child is expected to try out the role of speaker. Often Player A and Player B are both children; the roles of the adult are to temporarily fill in as speaker or listener, facilitate the children's communication, and otherwise monitor the playing of the game.

Program Characteristics

Recent research in language acquisition indicates that children learn to talk by having something to say in conversations with interested adults (Bloom, 1972; Cook-Gumperz, 1979). The games create situations that resemble conversational situations but that focus on and intensify certain characteristics of those situations. The specific features of the games are summarized below.

Information Transmission
In a game, there is information to be conveyed. The game situation, not the teacher, creates a demand for the use of language. In other words, there is a reason to talk other than to please the teacher; there is something that needs to be said. For example, the listener may need to know how the speaker has arranged a set of toys.

Reciprocal Roles
The child has the opportunity to encode and decode information. The child is not a passive responder, nor must the child always hold the floor. The children take turns playing the roles of speaker and listener, and the roles are complementary. The listener depends on the speaker to transmit needed information.

Contextual Support

The transmission of information takes place in a meaningful context, and the language demanded by the games involves the here and now of the playing materials. The players produce and comprehend utterances about materials they are using and seeing.

Feedback

The games provide the natural feedback of ordinary communicative situations. In the games, the reward is success in conveying information and not just success in pleasing the teacher. The games are structured in such a way that the child can perceive the adequacy or inadequacy of efforts to communicate.

Verbalization

The games create situations in which only words — verbal means of communication — are effective. For example, in some formats, a screen blocks each player's view of the other's toys. The rule to use words prevents the players from communicating nonverbally.

Specificity of Content

The games are used to teach specific content, not as all-purpose exercises in communication. One can teach specific vocabulary words, elicit specific kinds of grammatical constructions, and otherwise decide what to teach. In a game played with toys, for instance, including two different-colored dinosaurs creates a need to say *which* dinosaur is meant. Different props require the use of different syntactic devices. A bridge, for example, requires the use of locatives to specify whether characters are *on* or *under* the bridge.

Models

The child is not simply placed in a situation in which there is a need to use language. The games allow adults and other competent players to model effective language use. The adult provides model sentences as well as models of other aspects of language use. The child is thus provided with a model of *how* to use language to meet a specific need.

Practicality of Use

The games can be used by teachers, speech therapists, and others without a radical revision in their teaching styles or daily schedules. The games are adaptable to different settings, to different teaching styles, and to children with different needs.

Design for Young Children

Adults and older children who enter speech and language therapy supply their own contexts for work. They are motivated to improve because they understand that the way they talk affects other people's perceptions of them. Adults spend hours practicing the repetition of nonsense syllables if they understand that this practice is a means toward an end.

Young children do not make a sharp distinction between the means and the end; for them, the point of an activity is often the activity itself. Furthermore, unlike adults and older children, young children are generally not aware of their own language. Since they use language as a means of doing things and do not think about language in itself, activities must be intrinsically interesting.

Young children's interests differ radically from those of older children and adults. They are not interested in improving articulation for its own sake or in learning to produce agent plus action plus object constructions. They are not interested in improving their vocabularies simply to have larger vocabularies; rather, they are interested in playing with toys, socializing with peers and adults, and participating in activities for the sake of participation. Adults devote countless hours to pushing meaningless objects around game boards to win games and to develop interesting strategies to do so. Young children, in contrast, spend countless hours pushing things around if those things are fun to push around.

Perhaps more importantly, young, language-disabled children have needs in speech and language therapy that differ from those of adults and older children. The child whose productive vocabulary is limited to 20 words, the child who cannot ask for his favorite kind of cookie, the child who cannot verbally communicate his excitement about a fire engine, and the child who cannot even begin to converse with anyone outside his own family need to work on language that allow them to do those things. They do not need to pronounce words perfectly or use sophisticated verbal means to modulate meaning. The child who cannot say *potty* when he wants to go to the bathroom needs to learn to do just that. He does not need to pronounce *potty* perfectly or say *I want to go to the potty*. In other words, the child's immediate communicative needs should have priority over the fine points of articulation and grammar.

Opportunity to Use Language in Context

The single most important feature of the games is that they teach language in the context of meaningful use. Although a main goal of the program is to encourage children who are habitually silent to talk more, the games create the need to use words for specific purposes. They provide a reason and an opportunity to talk. The games are helpful in increasing vocabulary, but they build vocabulary not by teaching children to pair words and objects or pictures but by creating a reason to use one word for one object and another word for another object.

A unique strength of these games is their usefulness in eliciting grammatical constructions. The children are put in a situation in which there is a good reason to combine words. Syntactic skills are useful not because the teacher wants the child to say a given sentence but because the listener in the game needs to know several different but related pieces of information. Finally, the games create the need to use words to perform a variety of speech acts. The child is not taught to label pictures, then expected to generalize labeling pictures to requesting objects, asking questions, calling attention, and performing acts other than labeling.

Summary

The communication games differ from commonly used methods of language remediation by using communicative means to achieve communicative ends. The games are noncompetitive, referential, communicative tasks that create structured contexts for eliciting particular linguistic content. In playing the games, players alternate between the roles of speaker and listener. The speaker has information unavailable to the listener that the listener needs. The speaker must follow one basic rule: to use words to transmit information. The playing process begins with a check on the skills prerequisite to a particular game. One player then becomes the speaker. The listener makes a move in the game on the basis of the speaker's message. The players then receive feedback about the effectiveness of the communication by examining the materials used in the game. The players reverse roles, and the playing process continues.

The games intensify and focus on certain characteristics of conversation. The games are characterized by the transmission of information, reciprocal roles, contextual support, feedback, the need for verbalization, specificity of content, the provision of models, practicality of use in classrooms, design for young children, and the opportunity to use language in meaningful contexts.

2
Practical Assessment

This chapter is concerned with the process of assessing the individual child: Are the communication games appropriate for a particular child? What information should be available to plan a child's program?

Children with language disabilities are a heterogeneous group. Language disabilities include mild articulation disorders, a total lack of speech, delayed grammatical development, an inability to comprehend instructions, bizarrely disordered syntax, chronic silence in situations in which other children talk, articulation disorders so severe that the child's speech is incomprehensible, and so forth. A language disability may be a child's only presenting problem or may be only one of multiple problems. In undertaking work with a language-disabled child, it is important to know the exact nature of the language disability and to know about other disabilities the child may have. It is also important to gather other information about the child that may, at first glance, appear to be unrelated to the language disability.

In the assessment of a child's language ability and the formulation of program plans, consideration is often limited to the individual child without reference to the home and school contexts or the available teaching situations. In practice, decisions about a child's needs, strategies for meeting those needs, and specific plans for working with a child are always affected by the context in which the child lives. Children who test alike may differ in their needs because of their differing home environments. The child who has no opportunity for informal conversation with adults and the child who has extensive opportunity may appear alike when considered *in vacuo*, yet they have different needs. Children who attend communication-oriented classes have different needs from children who attend schools that provide little opportunity for communicative interaction. In assessing a child's appropriateness for a communicative language program, then, one must extend one's consideration to include the child's environment. Assessment must include the opportunities for communication that are already provided to the child.

In short, when deciding what one should do with a child, it is important to find out what is already being done and not being done. It is also important to distinguish between what one would like to do ideally and what one in fact has the opportunity to do. It is futile to decide that a child needs one-to-one work five days a week when the child is available only twice a week in a group of other children. This chapter presents a practical discussion of assessment. Rather than providing a set of criteria that bears no relationship to the situations in which one actually finds children with language disabilities, we provide some guidelines for assessment and program planning that consider the realities of these children's situations and the opportunities to work with the children within those realities.

Examining the Child's Record

Children referred for language and speech therapy have almost inevitably been examined and diagnosed at clinics or hospitals. Most have been given a range of standardized tests. One's task is not to reassess the child but to assess the child's potential to benefit from the communication games and to make decisions on how the games should be used with the child.

Information in the child's record is valuable for a number of reasons. First, the record may contain information that helps to orient one to the child. How old is the child? Is this child one of eight children? Is this child an only child? What is the child's living situation? Second, the record may contain diagnostic information. Does the child have Down's syndrome or some other syndrome? Does the child have handicaps that may affect his communicative behavior? This kind of information contributes to a realistic set of expectations about the progress the child will make and provides some initial guidelines about the cognitive skills the child may have. As discussed below, it is important not to accept diagnostic information as the absolute truth about the child; nevertheless, it should not be ignored. One must know whether a child is prone to seizures. One must also know whether the possibility of a cleft palate or malformation of the oral cavity has been explored. Third, a record may contain information about factors that complicate language and speech therapy.

While a child's record may be a source of valuable information, a record may also contain inaccurate information or contain important gaps. In particular, a record may indicate what has *not* been investigated. Consequently, it is important to examine a record with some skepticism.

With regard to the general accuracy of information, the best guideline is the sense one has of whether an assessment team actually paid close attention to the child. Records sometimes contain evidence that the writers of reports paid little or no attention to the child. For example, we worked with a 5-year-old boy named Hilary. Hilary was unmistakably a boy. He had a boy's haircut and wore boy's clothes. Nevertheless, the record contained several reports in which Hilary was consistently referred to as "she." Another child with whom we worked was extremely echolalic. Echolalia was, in fact, the single most obvious feature of the child's language handicap. This child's record, however, contained no reference whatsoever to the child's echolalia. Once one knows a child, one is able to recognize quickly the reports of people who have and have not paid attention to the child. Blatant inaccuracies and omissions in reports are not rare and are a sign that one should interpret the remaining information with considerable caution.

Information from tests should also be interpreted cautiously (Muma & Pierce, 1981.) The tests given to a child may have been inappropriate, and the testing itself may have been invalid. Many widely used tests are inappropriate for language-disabled preschoolers; they yield meaningless scores. For example, the Peabody Picture Vocabulary Test (Dunn, 1965) has been repeatedly criticized as a test for preschool children; yet it seems to remain a favorite for use with disabled preschoolers, perhaps because it is easy and straightforward to give and to score.

Finally, the record should be read for information about what was not investigated. In particular, we have often encountered records in which no data about hearing tests are presented. Undiagnosed hearing loss can produce a general picture very similar to language delay in a child with normal hearing. All too often, a record may indicate that the child's hearing could not be tested. If there is any reason to suspect any hearing loss, one must check the record carefully and, if no trustworthy information is available, have the child's hearing tested by a competent audiologist.

The importance of checking for factors that may interfere with the child's ability to speak cannot be emphasized enough. Some questions that must be answered prior to planning a program for any child are: Is there hearing loss or obstruction of the ear canal? Are there abnormalities or obstructions of the oral peripheral mechanism? Is there or has there been paralysis of the oral peripheral muscles? Is the language spoken at home the language of the school? Are there severe emotional problems that could account for the child's unwillingness to talk?

Information about complicating factors is important for three reasons. First, many problems can be corrected with appliances or surgery. Second, if the problem is permanent, teaching techniques that circumvent the difficulty must be devised. Third, a thorough understanding of complications unrelated to language acquisition greatly influences the goals that can realistically be set for the child.

Informal Observations of Nonlanguage Behavior

Observation of a child should begin in the child's natural environment, the classroom or, if possible, the home. Observation serves many functions. It provides an intuitive sense of "who this child is" and a familiarity with many characteristics of the child that affect decisions on therapy, such as whether to use the communication games and, if so, how to proceed. Observation should include attention to a number of factors, discussed below, as well as to language.

Temperament

Is the child cheerful or morose? Does the child sit passively for long periods? Will the child enjoy playing games in a fast-paced, exciting manner or a slow, deliberate manner? Will the child need the teacher or therapist to take a lively, energetic approach, or will the child be intimidated unless one approaches quietly and calmly?

Behavior Problems

Does the child show any behavior problems that are so disruptive that language work will be unproductive? Are there problems that will require special preparations and arrangements? Is it important to work with this child in a setting that will minimize disruptive behavior?

Attention

Does the child pay sustained attention to activities, or does the child seem unable to attend to anything for more than a few seconds? Does the child often seem to "tune out"? To what does the child pay attention?

Interests

Does the child display any particular interests in special toys or people? The child who seems to be without interests is, in some ways, the most difficult child with whom to work. A child's fascination with trucks or *Sesame Street* characters can provide a valuable clue to content that might engage the child in the communication games. Similarly, a child's attachment to another child in the class may suggest that the two children might work well together in the games.

Cognitive Ability

Observing the child in a natural setting may give information in the child's record. A child who is difficult to test may score low on standardized tests but show normal or nearly normal ability in everyday actions. In beginning to think about the games that might be appropriate for a child, one needs to investigate the child's ability to deal with pictorial representation. Does the child understand and enjoy pictures in books? Does the child use toys in fantasy play? Does the child use blocks to represent trucks, planes, and other objects? If there are photographs of the child's peers on a bulletin board, does the child recognize the people in the photographs?

Cultural and Family Background

Does the child have an air of neglect? Does the child seem accustomed to friendly approaches from adults? Do teachers comment on the extent to which the child's family supports the school's work? A child to whom the process of interacting with a friendly adult is unfamiliar requires considerably more time and input than a child to whom this process is familiar. Is it important to provide the child with experiences in ordinary, informal conversation? One sometimes encounters a child to whom no one ever seems to have addressed ordinary comments and questions. If the child seems to be neglected with regard to opportunities for conversation, it is important to provide these opportunities and to try to encourage others to do so as well.

Relationships with People

Does the child make eye contact? Does the child engage in group play with peers? Is the child isolated, shy, or outgoing? Does the child seek one-to-one contact with an adult? Does he avoid that contact? Does the child look longingly at groups of children but never join them? Does he have a stable friendship with another child? In what kinds of relationships does the child seem to be most comfortable or most uncomfortable? Is the child so aggressive with peers that playing the communication games with another child would be a miserable experience for the other child? Is there another child to whom the child might like to talk? Is the child unable to form any relationships with peers or adults?

Observation of Language Behavior

Children referred for language therapy or referred to language-focused preschools have often been given tests of language ability prior to placement in these settings. A large number of language tests are available for preschool children, and various books describe systematic ways to assess young children's articulation, vocabulary, syntactic, and pragmatic abilities. This section is not intended as yet another description of a system for testing or surveying the child's linguistic competence. Rather, it is a brief sketch of the kinds of information one may gain about the child's language from informal observation.

Language Comprehension

Language comprehension is difficult to assess in informal observation. What appears to be the comprehension of language may in fact be the comprehension of contextual cues rather than of the spoken word. For example, if a teacher tells a group of children to come to circle time, the child who immediately puts his toys away and marches off to the circle is not necessarily a child who has understood the teacher's words. He may be responding to his observations of other children's behavior or to his knowledge of the classroom schedule. Conversely, the child who does not respond to the teacher's instruction may have understood but may not want to comply. Informal observation can result in the overestimation or underestimation of a child's language comprehension abilities.

Despite these difficulties, children's misunderstandings are often quite evident. For example, children with comprehension difficulties sometimes produce inappropriate responses to the questions asked (e.g., Adult: "Do you want the red one or the blue one?" Child: "Yes.") Some children chronically engage in the kind of "yeah-saying" evident in this example. These children seem to discover that *yes* is a pleasant and welcome response and give affirmative replies without regard to the content addressed to them. Misunderstanding may also be evident when children are given directions and seem to think that they are complying even when they are not. For example, a child told to pick up a toy horse may always select a toy cow or may select animals at random. A child told to stand in back of something may stand in front of it.

While it is difficult to assess particular aspects of comprehension in informal observations, it is relatively easy to gain a sense of whether a child wants to understand what is said. Does the child seem interested in what others are trying to communicate? Does the child avoid being addressed? Is the receptive aspect of the child's intent to communicate evident?

Language Production

Language production, in contrast, is highly observable in informal observations. Of course, observation does not give full information about the child's ability to produce language — that is, about his or her underlying linguistic competence. It does, however, give information about how the child actually speaks in natural settings. There are many facets to language production evident when one observes a child in the classroom or at home. The following are some of the more obvious.

Amount of Speech
Does the child spend hours in the classroom without talking? Does the child seem to say as little as possible? Is the child garrulous? Does he take many or few conversational turns?

Length of Conversational Turns
When the child does say something, does he or she have a lot to say? Are most of the child's utterances very short? Does the child ever say more than one word at a time?

Comprehensibility
Is the child easy or difficult to understand? Does the child babble? Does the child speak too softly to be heard? Is the child's articulation poor enough to interfere with communication?

Vocabulary

Does the child use a highly restricted vocabulary or a relatively large vocabulary? Are the words used limited to a few nouns, relational words (e.g., *more*), and ritualized utterances? Does the child call all animals *horse*, use no verbs, and seem not to know the names of peers? Does the child use many verbs and many different nouns, prepositions, and adjectives?

Syntax

Does the child combine words to form two-word or multiword constructions? Are disorders evident in the child's syntax? Do the child's sentences seem scrambled or otherwise odd in construction?

Speech Acts

Does the child use language for many different functions, or is the child's use of language restricted to a few speech acts? Does the child use language mainly to label things? Does he or she ask questions? If so, what kind? Does the child direct the behavior of others? Does the child express propositions? Does he or she greet people, say good-bye, participate in ritualized classroom uses of language? What does the child do and not do with words?

Appropriateness

Is the child's use of language appropriate, or does it sound very odd? Is the child echolalic? Does the child immediately repeat what is said to him or her? Does the child show the delayed echolalia sometimes evident in autistic children?

Content

What does the child talk about? Is the content very odd? Does the child talk about the here and now, or does he also talk about past events? What about future events? Does the child constantly refer to "Mommy," or does he or she talk about interesting things in the classroom, peers, teachers, and events? Does the child talk about a range of subjects?

Conversational Skills

Does the child seem able to manage conversational interchanges? If an adult tries to have a conversation with the child, does the adult end up fulfilling most of the conversational functions? Does the child take his or her share of the conversational turns?

Context

In what contexts does the child talk most and least, best and worst? Does the child talk with peers but not with adults? Does the child talk with teachers but never with peers? Does the child talk during formal, structured activities but not in informal conversation? Does the child talk while engaging in fantasy play but not while working on task-related activities? Does the child remain silent in large groups but converse when in small groups?

Collecting Speech Samples

While informal observation is essential to gain an understanding of how the child actually uses language in everyday life, samples of spontaneous speech provide information that may not be evident in informal observation. Teachers are often strongly encouraged to collect samples of spontaneous speech to assess children's progress and plan programs. Our experience in classrooms suggests, however, that these samples often consist of isolated utterances and instances of unusual behavior. For example, if a child who practically never talks suddenly utters a surprisingly long sentence, the teacher may hasten to write the sentence down. When the child spends 3 hours without uttering a comprehensible word, that behavior may go unrecorded.

Collecting samples of spontaneous speech need not be a very time-consuming or bothersome process. The simplest way to collect these samples is to have one adult the child likes spend a few minutes talking and playing with the child while a tape recorder is running. For research purposes, particular stipulations may be placed on how long the talk goes on, when the samples are collected, and so forth, and one must go through the laborious process of transcribing the tapes. For clinical and teaching purposes, however, the tapes themselves may be used without further processing. When listening to a tape, the same sequence can be played again and again. One may notice many aspects of the child's use of language that are easy to miss when one is engaged in talking with a child. The tapes may confirm or disconfirm impressions gained while talking with the child. For example, a child who is adept at communicating nonverbally may leave the impression of a more adequate use of language than is evident when only the child's verbal output is available; the child who seemed talkative may have done a good deal of "talking" by using gestures and facial expressions rather than words.

Tapes may also be examined with particular questions about the child's needs in mind. For example, in the spontaneous speech samples, did the child ever use any verbs? What particular grammatical constructions did the child use? What sounds does the child produce perfectly? Are there sounds that the child seems utterly unable to produce? Does the child ever ask questions? Are most of the child's sentences imitations of sentences used by an adult?

Appropriateness of the Communication Games

Having gone through the process of learning about a particular child and about the child's language by reading the record, observing the child informally, and listening to samples of the child's speech, one is ready to decide whether the child might benefit from the communication games, and, if so, where to begin teaching. The criteria that make children inappropriate candidates for the communication games are presented below.

Serious Visual Impairment

Most of the games depend heavily on visual feedback. The child who cannot see objects, pictures, and people cannot gain the information needed to play.

Auditory Impairment that Interferes with Hearing Normal Conversation

If a child has an uncorrected hearing loss, the hearing loss should be corrected before work can begin.

Mild Articulation Disorders with No Other Language Handicaps Evident

Children with mild articulation disorders are inappropriate candidates for the program if their articulatory problems do not interfere with their ability to communicate. Vast numbers of preschool children articulate in an immature way. They are, after all, not yet mature people. These children may, however, participate as players with children who show other kinds of problems.

Certain Problems Not Involving Language

Children are sometimes referred for language work even though they show normal language development. Children who have a general air of neglect are sometimes assumed to have language handicaps. Children with orthopedic handicaps, emotional disturbances, and other handicaps not related to language sometimes end up in language-focused classrooms. These children make excellent players in the communication games, and they should be enlisted as players rather than as recipients of the program.

Absence of Communicative Intent

The rewards offered in the communication games are the rewards of communicating with other people. A child who does not find contact with people rewarding is an inappropriate candidate for these games. A severely mentally retarded child who tries to communicate neither gesturally nor vocally is not ready for these games. Autistic and autistic-like children may or may not benefit. In our work to date, we have played the communication games with only a few autistic children. Somewhat to our surprise, several of these children have seemed to benefit. At the present time, then, the appropriateness of this approach for autistic children is unclear.

Severely Disruptive Behavior

To play the games, a child must be able to pay attention without constantly scratching other people, spitting, running off, tearing things, and otherwise displaying serious behavior problems. A child with serious behavior problems is not ready for these games until the behavior problems are somewhat manageable.

Summary

The assessment of a child's potential to benefit from the communication games and decisions about the use of the games are based on information from the child's record, informal observations of behavior, and observations of language comprehension and production. The games are inappropriate for children with serious visual impairment, auditory impairment that interferes with hearing normal conversation, mild articulation disorders with no other evident language handicaps, certain problems not involving language, no evident interest in communicating, and severely disruptive behavior problems.

3
Which Games for
Which Child?

The games described in succeeding chapters are marked according to levels of increasing complexity. *Level I* refers to one-word utterances. The content of Level I games includes nouns, modifiers, verbs, quantifiers, and several other classes of words that can be used alone as utterances. *Level II* refers to two-word utterances. Level II games focus on simple combinations of elements from Level I, such as noun-verb constructions, noun-noun constructions, and so forth. *Level III* refers to multiword utterances and modulations. Level III games teach three-term and longer utterances and a variety of expressions used to make meaning highly explicit. These three levels may be subdivided in a way that facilitates program planning.

Level I games may or may not involve picture recognition skills and may or may not involve matching skills. Level I-A games involve neither of these skills. Level I-B games require picture recognition skills but not matching skills. Level I-C games require both skills.

Level II and III games are subdivided according to whether they are highly or loosely structured. The loosely structured games are, in general, somewhat more difficult than the highly structured games. Level II-A and III-A games are highly structured, while Level II-B and III-B games are loosely structured. Level III-C games are played without materials; they are word games, and hence are relatively demanding.

Table 1 shows the subdivisions of the levels. Each of the games described in this book is marked according to one of the sublevels in Table 1 or marked as an articulation game. Chapter 11 provides a discussion of each of these program levels and the content appropriately taught at each.

Table 1
Summary of Game Levels

Level	Description
I. one-word utterances	
I-A	no picture recognition or matching skills
I-B	picture recognition but no matching skills
I-C	picture recognition and matching skills
II. two-term constructions	
II-A	highly structured
II-B	loosely structured
III. multiword constructions and modulations	
III-A	highly structured
III-B	loosely structured
III-C	material-free word games

Achieving a Match

The communication games offer many different teaching options. They may be used to teach a variety of linguistic content and may be played by different arrangements of players. Different prerequisite skills are needed to play different games. The games also differ in format. The same basic game may be played using a variety of materials, and the same materials may be used to play games differing in format. Some games are highly structured, while others are relatively unstructured. A few games are played without materials.

Choosing among these options to achieve a good match between the child and the games requires consideration of the child's cognitive ability, temperament, interests, and other factors, in addition to a consideration of the child's strictly linguistic needs. In this chapter, we consider the process of achieving a good match between the child and the games. Fortunately, this process need not be complete before one begins to work with a child. Rather, in working with a child, one always monitors one's success in adapting the games to the changing needs of the child. A game that is perfect for a child in September may be inappropriate for him in November. Furthermore, the careful planning of a game for a child must always be tested against the observation of the child playing the game. A game intended to challenge a child may defeat him. A game intended to build a child's sense of himself as a competent speaker may bore him. The process of matching the child and the games, then, is inevitably one of trial and error.

Prerequisite Skills:
Picture Recognition and Matching

Many of the communication games have two specific skills as prerequisites: picture recognition skills and matching skills.

Children functioning at very low cognitive levels are sometimes unable to recognize photographs as representations. They seem to perceive photographs as patterns that may or may not be interesting, but not as patterns bearing a meaningful relationship to the objects photographed. Similarly, some children are unable to recognize drawings as depictions of objects. The extent to which a particular child has picture recognition skills seems to vary with the medium and with the content depicted. A child who seems to make nothing of a drawing of a cat may recognize a photograph of a cat as such. A child to whom a photograph of an unknown child is evidently a meaningless pattern may recognize his teacher in a photograph.

Picture recognition skills, then, are not an all-or-none phenomenon. In assessing whether or not a child has the picture recognition skills needed to play a game, it is necessary to check his ability against the particular materials to be used in that game. Level I-A games are played with objects rather than with drawings or photographs. These games, then, are suitable for children who generally have difficulty with picture recognition. Furthermore, these children may be able to play certain other games involving particular pictorial material. A child who seems generally to lack picture recognition skills might, for example, be checked for picture recognition skills with photographs of himself, photographs of peers, pictures of *Sesame Street* characters, drawings of Santa Claus, and other very familiar and appealing pictorial material.

Matching skills, like picture recognition skills, are not an all-or-none phenomenon. Different game formats involve different kinds of matching, some easier than others. It may be necessary to recognize that two objects are identical, that a picture matches an object, that two pictures are of the same object, or that two arrangements are the same. A child who has no trouble in matching simple pictures of animals may be unable to match arrangements of toys.

A child's performance on matching tasks in the games is sometimes complicated by attentional problems that interfere with matching ability. In particular, children sometimes attend to cues irrelevant to the task at hand. A child who is supposed to be checking to see whether a friend is sitting in a chair or standing next to the chair may ignore the friend's position relative to the chair while centering attention on whether or not the friend's hand is wide open or tightly shut. Children who have strong matching skills on many tasks, then, may still need help in inhibiting responses that interfere with their matching ability.

It is generally best to assess a child's matching ability for a game using the particular materials for that game. A child's performance with a highly motivating set of materials may be greatly in advance of his performance with a boring set of materials. On the other hand, a child's competence with one set of materials may vanish when the child is confronted with a set of overwhelmingly interesting toys.

Motor Skills

Children with Down's syndrome, neurological damage, and other handicapping conditions may lack the fine motor skills needed to manipulate the toys used in some games. A child whose fine motor skills are barely adequate may focus so much attention and effort on manipulating the toys that he is not free to attend to the linguistic aspects of the game. Consequently, children with serious difficulty in manipulating a set of toys should be given an alternative set that is easy to manipulate. Dolls that are somewhat difficult to pose may be replaced by dolls that are easier to pose. The placement of small toys in cars, under bridges, and in precarious positions is often difficult for these children. If it is impossible to find materials that are easy enough for the child to manipulate, it is usually possible to find a game format that does not involve manipulating toys but that teaches the same content. For example, a child who is unable to place toys on, under, and near a bridge in a Picture-Toy Matching Game (chapter 7) may be switched to the Picture Positions Action-Directive Game (chapter 9).

Cognitive Ability

A child's cognitive ability affects the choice of games in many ways. A child functioning at a low cognitive level must be given games involving a small number of objects. The objects must be introduced gradually. The concepts taught in a game must be kept relatively concrete. Some of the games discussed in succeeding chapters are cognitively demanding in that the players must be able to think up things to do; the children must be able to think up how to arrange toys, how to position themselves, or something similar. Children functioning at low cognitive levels need a great deal of practice in highly structured games and a great deal of exposure to appropriate linguistic models before they are ready for these challenging games. These children, then, are best exposed to Level I games and to Level II-A or III-A games before they play Level II-B or Level III-B games.

A child's cognitive ability affects the number of games he or she plays as well as the formats of games. A bright child may require a rapid pace; this child may play five or six different games in one session. He or she may use up a particular game after a small number of sessions. In contrast, the child with low cognitive ability may need to play the same game for all or most of a session and may need to keep playing a few games for many weeks or months. The rapid introduction of new materials, new variations on an old game, new formats, and other changes that keep a game interesting for a very bright child may bewilder and discourage a child with less ability.

Temperament and Interests

Children's abilities do not always match their interests. Children who could play games using the very demanding formats sometimes prefer simple formats. In particular, the Hiding Games described in chapter 5 seem to appeal to some children who could play more complicated games. These children seem to enjoy the excitement in the sudden revelation of the hidden object in a hiding game and seem not to require the explicit feedback provided by matching pictures or other materials available in other game formats.

Although, in general, it is best to use the formats a child prefers, children must sometimes be exposed to formats they find temperamentally jarring. In particular, passive children who never seem to use words to tell other people what to do or to initiate interaction can benefit greatly from playing games that require the speaker to issue directives and to ask questions, as in Action-Directive Games (chapter 9) and Guessing Games (chapter 10). In contrast, children who are easily overstimulated may be unable to handle the loose structure of Level II-B, III-B, and III-C games; a child who has chronic difficulty controlling his or her behavior may be unable to resist the impulse to toss together a heap of pictures and toys without attending to the point of a game.

Fortunately, a felicitous choice of materials is often effective in helping children to adjust their temperamental characteristics to the requirements of game formats. A child who loves fire engines is sometimes able to inhibit his or her hyperactivity to play a game about fire engines. A child who resists taking on the role of speaker in games requiring the speaker to issue directives may enjoy this role if he or she is amused by the silly actions the listeners are to perform. In contrast, the child who is wildly overstimulated when confronted with a set of dolls and vehicles may be able to play calmly with drawings of animals or with geometric shapes.

Perhaps the single most important temperamental characteristic of the child relevant to selecting games is the child's ability to tolerate communication difficulties. Some children are easily discouraged if listeners have trouble understanding them. Other children persist in trying over and over to get a message across even when the listener seems totally unable to grasp what these children mean. The former type of children must play many games that are relatively easy for them, while the latter type may rapidly progress to games that pose challenges. A child's willingness to persist in trying to convey a message, while influenced by temperament, is not necessarily fixed. The child who is easily discouraged when work begins may eventually learn that one really does want to understand him and that one's difficulty in decoding his messages does not interfere with one's affection for him or with one's continued interest in what he means.

Articulation

Although articulation is not a focus of the communication games, several games are available for direct work on articulation. Those games are marked accordingly in the following chapters.

Children with serious articulation disorders but with relatively advanced semantic, syntactic, and pragmatic skills sometimes benefit from playing games that are seemingly too easy for them. For example, the child who rapidly utters long but incomprehensible sentences may play very simple Level I games. This experience may help the child learn to monitor whether the listener correctly understands the speaker's message. Although the explicit linguistic content of these games may be very easy for such a child, making use of the listener's feedback may be difficult.

The bright child who is aware of his or her own serious articulation problems requires special consideration. It is important to avoid placing such a child in the humiliating position of being the only child in a group of players no one can understand. Rather, such a child may work best in one-to-one play with a supportive adult. The choice of game content may help the child to function as an effective speaker in groups: The group may use a game requiring the articulation of whatever sounds the child produces well. Thus, rather than choosing a game requiring the production of words with which the child has trouble, one does exactly the opposite by choosing a game that poses no challenge whatsoever. The experience of playing such a game may build the child's confidence so that he or she is ready to try a more difficult game.

In contrast, children who seem to be oblivious to the fact that others cannot understand them sometimes respond well to playing in groups of peers. The child to whom the message *I can't understand* is new may use this feedback to improve articulation. It is, however, important to monitor carefully the extent to which these children receive positive as well as negative feedback. The message *I understood that* must occur frequently.

Vocabulary

All of the game formats may be used to teach the comprehension and production of new words. When the goal is to increase a child's vocabulary in a specific content area, it is advisable to plan a number of different games involving the same concept. For example, preschools often teach units about zoo animals. These units are often integrated with a visit to a zoo and with the reading of books about zoo animals. To help children comprehend and produce names for zoo animals, many different formats and sets of materials are used. For example, a set of drawings of zoo animals could be used in Hiding Games With Pictures (chapter 5), and duplicate sets of those drawings could be used to play Lotto or Bingo (chapter 6). A different set of pictures could be used to play the same games. A set of small rubber animals together with photographs of those animals could be used to play a Picture-Toy Matching Game (chapter 7), and multiple sets of the rubber animals could be used in an Identical Arrangement Game (chapter 8). The point of using different materials and different formats is to help the child generalize what he or she learns to new materials and to new uses of words.

If the goal is to help a developmentally delayed, mainly nonverbal child to begin to use words, the simplest and most straightforward format to begin with is a Level I Hiding Game With Objects (chapter 5). For a child like this, one begins with what the child knows. For example, if the child has been heard to say *baby* and *car*, one could play a Hiding Game using a doll and a toy car. When the child started to produce those words in the game, one could introduce one new object, such as a "Mommy" doll to elicit *Mommy*. This tactic of introducing only one new thing at a time is appropriate for more advanced children as well; of course, the pace of introducing the new things may be rapid if a child quickly masters the new demands of the game. Teaching new vocabulary is effectively accomplished using Level I games, but

Level II and III games may be used to build vocabulary as well. For instance, in a Level II game, in which the primary purpose is to teach two-word combinations, one may also introduce the need to name new objects and actions. Indeed, some of the interesting and complicated Level II and III games involve toys that many children need help in learning to talk about. For example, the Superhero Games described in chapter 8 may require children to distinguish between dinosaurs that differ in color. Although the main purpose of this game is not to teach color terms, the game may accomplish that end.

Syntax

Level II and III games are designed to elicit, respectively, two-term and multiterm constructions. The design and use of these games is explained in detail in succeeding chapters. At this point, we stress one pitfall in selecting a game for teaching word combinations. Specifically, the teacher or therapist who is just beginning to use a communicative approach may try to use a Level I game to elicit two-term or multiterm constructions. For example, if the adult wants to help a child to comprehend and produce agent-action constructions, the adult might decide to use a Level I Hiding Game and might play this game using only two pictures — say, a picture of a man standing and a picture of a boy sitting. To refer uniquely to one of these pictures it is necessary to use only one word, not a two-word construction. *Man* or *stand* picks out the picture of the man standing, while *boy* or *sit* identifies the picture of the boy sitting. What is needed is a Level II game, that is, a game in which *man*, *boy*, *sit*, or *stand* alone would be ambiguous. A Hiding Game using pictures of the man standing, the man sitting, the boy standing, and the boy sitting would be the obvious choice. The experienced teacher or speech therapist is particularly warned to avoid the pitfall of selecting a lower level game than is required to elicit particular constructions.

The choice of Level II games is appropriate when a child is, in effect, "stuck" at the stage of producing only one word at a time. Level II games are also appropriate for children who produce only limited kinds of two-term constructions. For example, the child who uses agent-object and agent-action constructions frequently but who never seems to produce agent-locative constructions should play Level II games designed to elicit the latter. Simultaneously, this same child might play some Level III games designed to elicit agent-action-object constructions.

Amount of Speech

It might be argued that the single most obvious feature of the speech of language-disabled children is its rarity. Many language-disabled children spend hours in silence, either not communicating with people or communicating nonverbally. The failure to produce language is a particularly serious problem because these children's chronic silence deprives them of the opportunity to learn their native language by producing it.

Traditional models depicted language acquisition as a long period of passive comprehension finally followed by production. The child was envisioned as a vessel to be filled with language before spilling over into production. Newer approaches indicate that language acquisition is an active and interactive process. The child's production of words does not signal the child's mastery of the concepts those words convey to adults. Rather, children seem to learn what words mean partly by finding out what happens when they say them. A child who overgeneralizes the word *dog* to mean all animals discovers that *dog* is not an effective way to distinguish between a cat and a dog. Production, in short, generates feedback that helps children to further their construction of their native language. The child who hardly ever talks deprives himself of this learning opportunity.

The chronically silent child also deprives himself of exposure to the language of others. A child who hardly ever talks does not invite others to talk to him. Other people are apt to assume that such a child cannot understand what is said to him and that he will not respond; they do not address him in ways that provide models of language and do not stimulate him to produce language. The chronically silent child, in short, generates and contributes to a system that maintains his position as a nontalker. One of the main points of using a communicative approach to language remediation is to change that system.

Because all of the communication games have in common the *use words* rule, all are designed to impress upon the child the need to communicate verbally rather than nonverbally. This rule is also helpful to the adult who interacts with a chronically silent child, as these children often seem to invite the adult to avoid verbal communication. When playing the communication games, there is a structured, specific context in which to turn down that invitation.

When selecting games for these children, the particular materials chosen are in some ways more important than the format or game level. In commonsensical terms, the trick is to guess what the child would like to be able to talk about, then to give him the opportunity to do so. The selection of appropriate materials is best guided by careful observations of what does and does not interest the child in his everyday life. On the rare occasions on which the child speaks, what does he talk about? If the child practically never says anything except *no*, one might play a Hiding Game in which one simply addresses yes-no questions to the child. If the child occasionally produces the name of an animal, one might play a Lotto Game with pictures of the animals the child has mentioned. In other words, instead of trying to force the child to produce words one does not know that he can say, one concentrates on providing the child with the opportunity to say what he can say. Once the child begins to use words in the games, the games can be selected on the basis of the child's need for work on syntax, vocabulary, or other linguistic content. To place a chronically silent child in a situation that immediately challenges his tenuous ability to talk is counterproductive. The point is to make it easy, not difficult, for such a child to speak.

Performance of Speech Acts

To understand the use of the communication games in facilitating the development of children's ability to use language to perform a variety of functions, a brief digression into the theory of speech acts is necessary. The philosopher Austin (1962) described utterances as three different kinds of acts. A locutionary act is an act of saying something. An illocutionary act is the performance of an act in saying something. A perlocutionary act is the achievement of certain ends by saying something. To say something is to perform a locutionary act; to argue something is to perform an illocutionary act; to convince someone is to perform a perlocutionary act. Austin argued that all utterances have illocutionary force as well as locutionary meaning: "To say something *is* to do something, or *in* saying something we do something, and even *by* saying something we do something." (1962, p. 94)

Traditional methods of language remediation concentrate on the locutionary aspects of utterances and limit themselves mainly to the one illocutionary act of labeling. The point of most methods of language remediation is to have children say things, not to have them "do things with words," to use Austin's phrase. In contrast, the communication games create situations in which the saying of something is the doing of something and has some kind of effect. When a child in traditional therapy is shown a picture and told to say *cat*, his utterance of *cat* has illocutionary force and perlocutionary effect. He performs the acts of labeling the picture and complying with a demand. His utterance has the effect of gratifying the person who asked him to say *cat*. The content of the child's utterance, however, bears no meaningful relationship to its illocutionary force or perlocutionary effect. The communication games, in contrast, create contexts in which the child's utterance of a word—*cat* for instance—has an illocutionary force besides labeling and a perlocutionary effect beyond the gratification of the trainer. When the child says *cat*, he issues an order, asks a question, agrees, disagrees, or does something else—something that has to do with cats. The child's utterance also has a perlocutionary effect: It leads the listener to lift up a picture, move toys around, reply to a question, or to do something else about cats.

The practical point emerging from this digression is that the communication games must be selected and used in such a way that the child has as great an opportunity as possible to do things by saying things. The teacher or speech therapist with traditional training has been explicitly taught to focus on the locutionary aspect of utterances and to elicit utterances with the one illocutionary force of labeling things. In playing the communication games, it is imperative to avoid those limitations.

The game formats themselves differ somewhat in the demands they create for different kinds of speech acts. In particular, Action-Directive Games (chapter 9) focus heavily on the elicitation of directives, while Guessing Games (chapter 10) necessitate the use of questions. The need to use language for many purposes arises, however, in all formats. For example, the listener who does not understand the speaker's utterance needs to request clarification, regardless of what communication game the two are playing. In all of the games, the speaker's description of an object, picture, or arrangement serves to command the listener to do something. The game formats and games differ mainly in how explicit the speaker must be in performing an act.

Furthermore, different formats seem to be more or less effective, in a seemingly idiosyncratic way, in eliciting a variety of speech acts from children. For example, the Superheroes and Dinosaurs Game (chapter 8) seems to be very effective in eliciting requests for clarification and questions from some children. The much simpler Hiding Games (chapter 5) seem to serve this same function for other children. In general, the more unstructured a game, the more opportunity it provides for a variety of uses of language; the loosely structured games are, in general, more like everyday conversations than are the highly structured games.

When selecting games, then, both the systematic and idiosyncratic effects of the games on the elicitation of speech acts should be considered. First, children who do not ask questions are exposed to Guessing Games (chapter 10) that necessitate the use of questions, and children who do not use words to give orders are exposed to Action-Directive Games (chapter 9), in which the connection between saying something and having someone do something is dramatic. Second, the best way to provide a wide range of opportunities for the use of a variety of speech acts is to expose a child to a variety of formats and to observe the child's idiosyncratic responses to those formats. Third, children should be given loosely structured games (Level II-B and III-B) when these games are appropriate in other respects. That is, a child who initially needs the structure of Level II-A or III-A games should be moved to a more loosely structured game as soon as he or she is able to handle the freer situation.

Self-Image and Self-Esteem

A child's language handicap is sometimes part of a self-perpetuating personality system involving the child's self-image and self-esteem. In particular, the child with normal or high intelligence who continues to have difficulties in speaking into his fifth or sixth year sometimes radiates the conviction that talking can result only in failure. A lack of confidence in one's power to use words to communicate is not limited to those children who display it in an apparently self-conscious way. Children with language disabilities are, after all, children who have actually had repeated experiences of failure as speakers and, often, as listeners. As discussed previously, some children persist in their efforts to communicate despite repeated communication failures, while others seem to have given up on talking before one encounters them. When selecting the games a child will play, it is important to consider the potential effects of a game on his self-image — specifically, on his feelings about himself as a communicator.

One way to give the child experiences in communicating that help to build self-image and self-esteem is obviously to give the child games that he will play competently. The pitfall of this tactic is that one may simply bore the child. A more successful tactic is to give the child a game that he can master easily but that he is not immediately capable of playing competently. Another tactic is to use a game with timely content. For example, Halloween and other holiday games may be very easy for children but may nevertheless interest them and provide them with the experience of success. Another tactic is to let the child who has mastered a game play that game with a beginner, that is, to transform the habitually incompetent pupil into a competent peer-tutor for another child.

Games may also be selected for content that helps the child to impress teachers, parents, and others with his verbal proficiency. The particular content useful in this way varies from school to school and from subculture to subculture. Some schools and some families place a high value on a child's knowing color terms and being able to count. While a knowledge of color and number terms is not one of the child's most pressing needs, the child's ability to show himself off as a person who knows numbers and colors may have significant effects on how important people in his environment react to him. Similarly, a child's ability to talk about Santa Claus, Big Bird, cartoon characters, and other inhabitants of popular culture may enable him to attract conversants who might otherwise ignore him.

Recognizing Success and Failure

The most obvious sign that a game is the right one is a child's pleasure in playing it. In particular, successful games are games that children request spontaneously. Another sign of success is the amount of speech a child produces while playing; a game that generates a great deal of talk is a game that is working well. Finally, a game is successful if the child is obviously working hard to play it — the child is not struggling but is attending to the game and clearly trying to do something new.

Unsuccessful games or games that have lost their usefulness are often signaled by signs of boredom. Boredom may indicate that a child is tired of a particular game, that a child simply dislikes a game, that a game is too easy, or that it is too difficult. Similarly, fidgeting and misbehavior are signs that something is amiss. Boredom, fidgeting, and misbehavior are temptingly easy to interpret as signs that the child has problems rather than as signs that one should be doing something different. A child may act bored and restless and may misbehave when he is not challenged by the games, unhappy in one-to-one work, defeated by the difficulty of the games, embarrassed to display his difficulty in groups of peers, or for other reasons that can be corrected by changing the games the child plays, the arrangement of players, or both.

While boredom, fidgeting, and misbehavior may signal that the games a child is using are too easy or too difficult, the child's silence or an air of defeat and discouragement almost always mean that the games are too difficult for the child. In considering what to do differently, one sometimes ignores the simple answers that the wrong games or the wrong arrangements of players are being used. While one's attitude toward a child, one's style, and other interpersonal factors may, of course, create serious problems that emerge as fidgeting, boredom, and misbehavior in the child, the simple solutions of providing the child with different games or placing him in a different playing situation should be tried before one searches for hidden causes and subtle solutions.

Summary

The explicit content of the program is divided into three levels. Level I consists of one-word utterances, such as nouns, color terms, and quantifiers. Level II games teach two-word constructions, such as agent-object, agent-locative, and attribute-entity constructions. Level III games teach multiword constructions and certain devices for modulating meaning; agent-action-object contructions, the meaningful use of prepositions, and contrastive word order are examples.

Each level of game is subdivided. Level I-A games require neither picture recognition nor matching skills. Level I-B games require picture recognition skills but not matching skills. Level I-C games require both picture recognition and matching skills. Level II-A and III-A games are highly structured; Level II-B and III-B games are loosely structured. Level III-C games are word games played without materials.

Achieving a good match between the child and the games is a trial-and-error process. When selecting games, it is important to consider the child's picture recognition, matching, and fine motor skills; cognitive ability; temperament and interests; articulation; syntax; amount of speech; performance of speech acts; and self-image and self-esteem. The child's interest, requests for games, talkativeness, and effort signal a good match. Boredom, fidgeting, and misbehavior may indicate that a game is either too easy or too difficult, while silence and an air of defeat usually mean that easier games should be used.

4
Player Arrangements and Structural Maneuvers

Most of the communication games described in this book may be played by one adult and one child, by pairs of children supervised by an adult, and by small groups of children. One child may sometimes play alone with an adult, sometimes with another child, and sometimes in a small group. When determining the best of these arrangements for a particular child, various advantages and disadvantages of the arrangements must be considered.

Individual Work

One-to-one play with an adult is useful to teach a child a new game format. In this arrangement, the adult is free to focus all of his or her attention on one child and to make sure that the child is mastering the new game format.

This arrangement is also appropriate in other circumstances. A child with behavior problems, especially a child who may be aggressive toward peers, must work individually or not at all if other children are to have happy experiences in playing. An emotionally needy child may thrive on the exclusive attention of an adult. Finally, children with very serious difficulties may require undiverted attention. These kinds of difficulties may or may not be language-specific. A chronically silent child who seems to have an emotional resistance to talking may benefit from individual work. A child with marked cognitive delay, emotional withdrawal, and delayed language may be unable to function in a group.

Structural Maneuvers for Individual Work

Structural maneuvers are devices for positioning oneself physically and interpersonally to reflect and define the psychological distance between the adult and the child. In one-to-one work, the adult has three options: The child may be next to the adult, facing the adult, or in the adult's lap.

When the adult and the child sit opposite one another, particularly when they sit on opposite sides of a table, the child is in a relatively autonomous position. In contrast, positioning oneself next to the child helps to define a collaborative or cooperative relationship. Holding the child in one's lap contributes to a somewhat fused relationship. The use of spatial position has implications for the affective tone of the situation; it is easier to put an arm around a child if the child is nearby instead of far away. In addition, the closer one is to the child and to the playing materials, the greater the possibility and ease of control. Subtly, it is easier to prevent a child from breaking the *use words* rule of the games when the child and the materials are within reach than when they are not.

Spatial distance between oneself and the child is something one can always change. A child accustomed to working opposite a teacher at a table need not continue to do so, and a child who customarily sits on the teacher's lap can be moved to a more distant position. Furthermore, the adult may arrange changes in spatial position during the course of a single playing session.

Changes in seating arrangements are useful to help children experience uses of language in the different interpersonal contexts the seating arrangements define. Changes in seating may also serve some more specific purposes. First, the teacher may increase or relax control by changing seating arrangements. Second, seating changes may help define one's interpersonal relationship with the child. The passive or dependent child who prefers to loll in someone's lap may function more capably in a distant position. In contrast, a distant child who avoids eye contact and otherwise relates poorly may benefit from being moved physically closer.

Actually accomplishing these changes in seating position is simple and casual. One can say, "How about sitting in my lap?" or "Now it's time for you to sit here." An alternative is to do the moving oneself; simply to move opposite or next to the child. There is no reason to make a big deal about changing seating positions.

Group Work

Two Adults with One Child

In exceptional circumstances, it is sometimes useful to conduct a few sessions with two adults and one child. This arrangement is necessary when a child functioning at a very low cognitive level seems utterly unable to grasp the basic ideas of even the simplest games. When two adults are present, the playing situation becomes failure-proof. One adult holds the child and plays for the child, while the other adult acts as the other player. The child is gently forced to experience the game the way it is supposed to be played. The players (the adult and the adult-child pair) take turns, talk, and respond smoothly and correctly. In other words, the child is given a simple model of how he or she is supposed to act.

One Adult with Two Children

In this arrangement, the adult may serve many different functions. The adult may supervise the children, enacting a facilitative role but not actually playing. The adult may play as a unit with one of the children. The adult may step in and out of the play, occasionally taking a turn to model some use of language.

It is sometimes desirable to work regularly with pairs of children — that is, always or often to work with Child A and Child B together. Although the pairing of children is an important issue on which a set of hard and fast rules would be helpful, no such rules seem to be valid. Certain kinds of pairings never work. A child who hurts other children should never be allowed to inflict injury on other players. Pairing a very assertive, dominant child with a very withdrawn and passive child is usually unproductive, as the assertive child drowns out the other child. Certain children seem to elicit only silly, regressive behavior from one another. Finally, some children simply dislike each other. If one finds that pairs like these have been formed, the pairs should be broken up immediately.

Forming pairs of children is best guided by observation of children in spontaneous interaction. Two children may have a fairly stable friendship and may enjoy playing together. Sometimes one child shows a great deal of unrequited admiration for another child; the admired child may be induced to play and may enjoy the adult attention, the process of playing, and other aspects of the games, while the admiring child enjoys being with his or her hero.

It is sometimes helpful to a child to be paired with another child functioning at a much lower linguistic level. A child with language disabilities seldom has the opportunity to be the more competent of two conversants. A child who spends most of his or her life functioning as an incompetent speaker may benefit from the rare opportunity to show off superior communication skills.

When forming pairs of children, one often does best simply by trying out pairs and observing what happens. Pairings that seem unlikely sometimes work. For example, we were working with two boys who attended the same class but who seldom interacted with one another in the classroom. One child was extremely echolalic. He made no eye contact with people, and when he talked about the pictures and objects used in the games he stared off into space instead of looking at whatever he was talking about. His cognitive development seemed to be very delayed. The other child was very friendly, cheerful, and engaging. He talked a great deal but showed peculiar and disordered syntax and word substitutions (e.g., "a number cat" to mean *two cats*). There was no reason to suppose that these children, with very different problems and personalities and with no history of friendship, would benefit from playing together. One day, however, their language therapist realized that she had time to see only one of the two children; she decided, instead, to work with this unlikely pair. The combination worked very well. Although she feared briefly that the echolalic child would echo the other's disordered syntax, this did not happen. The boys enjoyed being together. The echolalic child, in fact, began to direct nonecholalic communications to the other boy, who seemed to make efforts to make his talk communicative.

Structural Maneuvers for Dyads and Small Groups

The maneuvers used in one-to-one work also may be used with dyads and small groups, but the presence of two or more children makes additional maneuvers possible.

Joining

To "join" with a child is to share the speaker or listener role with that child. The adult and child play as a single unit. The nonverbal signal of joining is physical proximity; the adult holds the child or sits very close to him.

This maneuver is useful when working with a group containing several relatively able children and one child unable to participate at their level. The task of the adult is to allow that child to do as much as possible and to model the remainder. The child with whom an adult successfully joins in a role has the vicarious experience of competence and success and is provided with accessible models of successful language use.

Alternating

The child and adult alternate in a role when sometimes one and sometimes the other takes the role. Typically, the child is the principal actor while the adult steps in occasionally. The adult is usually next to or behind the child for whom he or she is alternating.

Alternating is useful when a child seems about to be overwhelmed by the difficulties of a game, but it is not reserved for rescue operations. It is particularly useful when introducing new models and variations of games. For example, if two children playing an Identical Arrangement or Directive Game are bogged down in monotonous material (e.g., the only actions being used are to sit and to stand), the adult, as alternate speaker, may step in to make a superhero doll fly or to introduce jumping.

Fading Out

Fading out occurs when the adult actively performs some function, then gradually reduces the frequency of his or her participation. This process is usually marked by a physical withdrawal from the group; the adult sits back or moves slightly to the periphery of the group.

Creating a Vacuum

The adult creates a vacuum by actively and strongly enacting a role, then abruptly turning the role over to a child. In particular, the adult may be a highly visible, lively, and entertaining speaker; moving to the periphery of the group, he then announces, "It's Jim's turn." When this maneuver is successful, the children sustain the lively atmosphere and pace the adult has created.

Two Adults and Two Children: "Visits"

If two adults are working individually with children, the adults and children may sometimes "visit" one another. That is, the two adult-child dyads may meet together. This kind of visiting may help prepare the children for work in pairs with other children. It may also give children who require individual work an opportunity to communicate with other children in a highly structured and supportive context.

One Adult with a Group of Children

Not all of the communication games are suitable for use with a group. Lotto, Bingo, and Hiding Games are, however, adaptable for group play. Groups of four or five children can generate a sense of conviviality and excitement difficult to create in a smaller group. Furthermore, these groups help children experience the same kinds of demands for language they experience at snack time, in circle time, and in other classroom situations. With the help of the adult, a child unable to participate in circle-time activities has the opportunity to participate in a small group. Children functioning at low cognitive and linguistic levels cannot, of course, keep up with the more advanced children in a small group. While they may not understand the basic ideas of the games that engage the group, they may nevertheless find the group experience motivating. They can observe the other children, who provide good models of language use. They have some chance to participate in interchanges in groups if the adult provides plentiful prompting and encouragement.

If nonhandicapped or relatively advanced children are included in a group, it might seem that only relatively challenging games could be used. This is not the case. The interest generated by the process of playing in the group seems to override the nonchallenging nature of the games. There are many advantages to including these able children in a group. They provide good models for the other children. They understand and enforce rules clearly. Since they are able to play with minimal help from the adult, the adult is free to devote attention to the children who need help. Finally, an enjoyable group experience may help these advanced children come to know their less able peers and may facilitate the development of relationships among the children in everyday interactions.

Practical Notes

The teacher or therapist may have firm ideas about the ideal arrangement for working with a child yet may find that practical considerations dictate another arrangement. One may be assigned many children to see in a brief time. A school may insist that a child have one-to-one work. One may decide that two children should work together, only to discover that one of the two children is absent from school most of the time. We have repeatedly had the experience of placing children in working arrangements that we would not, a priori, have chosen, only to find that these arrangements have advantages we failed to foresee. Arrangements based on necessity sometimes work much better than one would predict.

Choosing an Arrangement

When one has the freedom to choose the arrangements of players, that choice should not, in general, mean placing a child in only one arrangement. In playing the games, the child has the opportunity to address a small audience and to be a member of one. If the child works in only one dyad or small group, the child has no opportunity to use the communication games as a way to expand his or her audience. Different players make different communicative demands as speakers and as listeners. By changing the children's exposure to listeners and speakers, one can help them increase the range of people with whom they can communicate.

The only warning about providing a range of audiences is not to bewilder the child. In particular, children who are easily disoriented or made anxious by transitions and by changes in structure may need stable, predictable arrangements. In general, one needs to help young children anticipate and deal with changes. For example, if a child-therapist dyad is to visit another dyad, each therapist should prepare his or her child for the visit. The child can be helped to anticipate what will happen (e.g., *Next time we play, we're going to play with....*).

Selecting a Location

The location for the communication games is not always something one has the freedom to choose. A language and speech therapist assigned to one room may not be welcome elsewhere in the school. If, however, different options are available, the advantages and disadvantages of the options should be considered.

Except in unusual circumstances, the preferred place to work is in the child's own classroom. In the classroom, children are in a familiar environment and in one of the environments in which they need to use language. They do not receive the covert message that communicating clearly and effectively is something to do in a special place. More importantly, in the classroom the child may easily play the games with a variety of classmates; peers may wander into the playing area, nondisabled children may be enlisted as players, and teachers may join the group. However, the classroom may be too noisy to play the games effectively or too crowded to permit playing without numerous interruptions and distractions. The teachers may find that one more activity taking place in the room is intrusive. A very distractible child may need the quiet and calm of a space outside the classroom.

Whether one is working inside or outside the classroom, the space for playing the game must be defined. The players may sit at a table or on the floor, or they may use various props, like chairs and tables, in the games. If the only available space is a room filled with distracting materials, it is helpful to use a rug or a series of rugs as a means of defining the space; the child may be told that the games are played only when everyone is on the rug. Regardless of whether the games are played at a table or on the floor, all players must be comfortable. A teacher who prefers the formality of a table should not force himself or herself to sprawl on the floor. If the players are seated at a table, however, the adult must avoid sitting in an adult-size chair several feet above the children; rather the adult should be at eye level or close to eye level with the children.

Summary

The communication games may be played on a one-to-one basis and in small groups. Various combinations of adult and child players may participate. Arrangements of players and locations for playing may be adapted to the needs of children and to the requirements for effective work. Selections of players and the use of spatial arrangements help define the psychological relationships among the players; thus, varying the composition of groups and changing seating positions may be used as maneuvers for facilitating children's participation in the games.

5
Hiding Games

Hiding Games are simple guessing games. One player hides an object, and another player or players guesses the location of the hidden object. These games are useful in introducing children to the basic rules of the communication games. They are relatively undemanding, yet fun; children with very small vocabularies can succeed if the games are designed properly. In the Hiding Games first described, a small object is hidden under a large object or concealed in the hands or clothing of the players. In the Hiding Games later described, a small, flat object is hidden under one of a series of pictures.

Hiding Games with Objects

Prerequisite Skills

Hiding Games with Objects require neither picture recognition nor matching skills. If a child can give even minimal attention, these games are appropriate.

49

Players

Most of these games may be played by one adult and one child. When introducing these games to children functioning at a low cognitive level or to children whose distractibility or impulsiveness is a problem, it is effective to begin by playing with two adults and one child. Many children can begin by playing in dyads or small groups.

"Who Has...?" (Level I-A)

The purpose of this game is to help children comprehend and produce the names of the children and adults in their class. Three players are needed.

Materials
The only material required is a small and interesting object. For example, a game of "Who has Superman?" may be played using a small Superman doll. Other appropriate objects include small rubber animals and dolls — virtually anything small enough for children to hide by holding the object behind their backs or tucking it into a pocket. At holiday times, a small toy Santa Claus, pumpkin, Easter bunny, or other seasonal toy may be used.

Because "Who has...?" games are useful mainly with children functioning at very low cognitive and linguistic levels, the children for whom a "Who has...?" game is appropriate may often mouth objects. Consequently, it is *imperative* to use toys that are too big to swallow or to lodge in the larynx and to use toys that are nontoxic. Do not use toys with small parts that can break off, toys with paint that may peel off, or toys that could in any other way be dangerous.

How to Play
The speaker closes his eyes. One of the other two players hides the object by putting it behind his back, tucking it into a sweater, putting it in a pocket, holding it in his hands, or by concealing it somewhere else. The speaker is then told to open his eyes and to guess who has the toy (e.g., *OK. Ready. Open your eyes. Now, who has Superman?*).

If the speaker does not produce the name of one of the players, several kinds of prompts may be used. The adult model guesses by saying, for example, "Mary or Billy? Mary? Billy?" The child's repetition of either of the names is interpreted as a valid guess. Alternatively, the adult may transform the question into a yes-no question, asking, for instance: "Does Mary have Superman? Mary?" In this case, a yes or no response is interpreted as valid.

The only rule in this game is that guesses must be verbal. Pointing to a person, reaching out to look for the toy, and otherwise guessing nonverbally is not allowed. The simplest way to communicate this rule is to hold the child in one's lap or to hold the child's hands when it is the child's turn to guess.

Nonverbal children may play this game if one interprets *vocal* responses as valid verbal responses. The most effective way to do this is to interpret the vocalization as the name it most closely approximates. For instance, if the child produces a "b" sound and one of the players has a name containing that sound, one treats the vocalization as an approximation of that person's name.

This game demands only the production of a sound that allows one to distinguish among the players who might have the hidden object. If one can tell which player the child means when he speaks, then one should not ask for further verbalization. It is important not to ask for improved articulation unless one cannot understand the child's meaning. It is also important not to ask for full sentences or phrases. Do *not* ask the child to say: *Jenny has Superman, Jenny has it, I guess Jenny*, or anything not required to play the game.

As soon as the speaker produces the name of one of the other players, that player responds either by showing the object or by indicating that he does not have it. When the speaker guesses correctly, the adult player or players uses that as an opportunity to model the use of names. (*Yes, Mary had Superman. Mary. You said "Mary," and Mary had Superman.*) Similar modeling may be used even when the child does not guess correctly (e.g., *Not Billy; Billy doesn't have Superman this time. Billy doesn't. Maybe Mary has Superman.*).

After the child has succeeded in locating the hidden toy, it is someone else's turn to be the speaker. For children just beginning to play the communication games, the switching of turns may be emphasized. (*Now it's Billy's turn to close his eyes.*) After taking one turn closing his eyes and trying to locate the object, a child may immediately assume that he always plays in that way. It is important to begin taking turns immediately to prevent difficulty later in conveying the idea that one does not always close one's eyes while playing this game.

The play continues as described above with the new player covering or closing his eyes, then guessing who has the object.

Two-Player Version

If one is playing with a very low-functioning child, it may be useful to structure the game so that there is only one person who can have the hidden toy. Specifically, if an adult is working alone with the child, the adult must have the hidden object. Consequently, *anything* the child says may be interpreted as a valid and correct guess. This very rudimentary game is useful with children who produce mainly uninterpretable vocalizations. It provides a context in which vocalizations are interpretable as meaningful and hence helps the child connect the act of vocalizing with an interesting result.

Eyes-Open Version

There are several circumstances in which it is desirable to play "Who has...?" without first asking the speaker to close his eyes. First, children functioning at an extremely low cognitive level may initially miss the point of the game. They may not get the idea that they are supposed to *guess* where the object is hidden. Once the object is out of sight, it may be out of mind as well, cognitively or attentionally. Second, autistic and autistic-like children may become distressed about closing or covering their eyes.

Although the eyes-open version is pointless to an adult, it is not necessarily pointless to children. The child may forget the location of the object even when he has seen it hidden. The child may also enjoy the process of playing even when he already knows where the object is. The point, for the child, may be the appearance of the object regardless of all other considerations.

Two-Adults, Two-Children Version

When working with two children functioning at very low cognitive and linguistic levels, it may be helpful to play "Who has...?" with two adults. Each adult holds a child in his or her lap. One adult-child dyad guesses collectively which of the other two players has the object. The adult in the other dyad manages the process of hiding the object, providing responses, and so forth. In this version, adults totally structure and control the game, so the playing process goes smoothly, and the children see the way the game is supposed to be played. The game is failure-proof. In addition, the adults not only model the process of playing but also model the rules of the game and the language needed for the game. For instance, the adult playing the role of speaker can cover his or her eyes while simultaneously covering the eyes of the child he or she is holding. When the other speakers are instructed to look, the adult uncovers the child's eyes and makes a big point of guessing verbally, not reaching out and trying to grab the other players.

Objects Under Objects (Level I-A)

Instead of having other players hide a small object, one may hide the object under one of a set of specified larger objects. The purpose of this kind of game is to help the children use the names of the larger objects under which the small object is hidden.

Materials

The small object to be hidden may be the same object used in "Who has...?". As in those games, any small, interesting, and safe object is suitable.

The larger objects should be attractive and familiar to the children. They must be large enough to hide the small object. Large dolls, stuffed animals, pillows, small rugs, and various other objects found in a classroom are suitable. It is desirable to choose larger objects whose names will be immediately useful to the children. For example, if the children sit on small individual rugs during circle time and are frequently told to get their rugs, to put their rugs away, to sit on their rugs, and so forth, then a rug is an appropriate object.

For a low-functioning child, one larger object may be enough. If two objects are used, they are selected so that one of them is something the child can already name, while the other is something the child evidently cannot name. For more advanced children, three or four objects may be used.

How to Play

The speaker closes or covers his eyes while a listener hides the small object under one of the larger objects. When the small object is hidden, the listener announces that he or she is ready (e.g., *Ready.* or *Open your eyes.* or *You can look now.*). The speaker then tries to locate the hidden object by guessing the object under which it is hidden. When he succeeds, it is his turn to hide the small object.

As in "Who has...?", children who are inclined to guess by reaching for the larger objects, pointing, or otherwise guessing nonverbally may be gently restrained. The adult playing with one child may hold the child while gently hugging his or her arms. The players may hold hands while the guessing goes on. When it is the adult's turn to guess, the adult may make a big point of guessing verbally and not pointing or touching the objects.

Note that different words may be equally effective as guesses in this game. For example, if one of the larger objects used in the game is a doll, then *dolly*, *baby*, *girl*, and other terms may be equally effective in telling a player to look under the doll rather than under the other toy or toys used in the game. Any word that works is acceptable. One does not insist that the child say *doll*, *baby*, or any other particular word. If the child's word lets one know where to look for the hidden object, then the child has communicated sucessfully, and there is no reason to ask the child to use a different word. If one wants the child to produce a word other than the one he has produced, one must create a game in which that word is needed.

Two-Adults, Two-Children Version

This game may be played with two sets of players: one adult and child who play together as the hiders, and one adult and child who play together as the guessers. In this version, the adults control and model the playing as needed. The adults may gradually fade out of the picture, turning the playing over to the children as they begin to catch on to the idea of the game.

Modifier Versions

Hiding Games with Objects may be used to teach modifiers as well as nouns. To teach the use of modifiers, one selects two toys that are different versions of the same object, such as a big doll and a small doll. The contrast should be clear and sharp: Big must be very big. In this case, the player guessing the location of the object must specify the big or the small doll. It is *not* necessary to use a noun; the speaker need not say, for example, *big doll* or *small doll*. The modifier alone is effective communicatively.

Color Terms

The use of color terms is a special case of the use of modifiers. One selects two objects that differ only in color. Each should be only one color. For example, if one wants to teach the words *red* and *blue*, each object should be unicolor. A red truck with green wheels will not do. The colors themselves should be clear, bright, and distinct. The red, for example, should be red, not even vaguely orange or pink. Disposable plastic cups are useful in creating this kind of color game. The cups, approximately 4 inches high, are available in several colors, but it is inexpensive and simple to buy a set of white ones to color as needed with magic markers.

One begins by using only two of the colored cups. The colors must be very different: red and white, red and blue, and so forth — *not* green and blue or red and orange. A small toy is hidden under one of the cups, and the speaker guesses where the toy is by naming the color of the cup where he would like the listener to look. Notice that to succeed in this game, the child need not produce the color terms accurately. If, for example, the child uses *red* as a generic word for color (or uses *red* to refer to red, orange, and yellow), he can still succeed if a red cup is one of the options. The child will, in fact, have the experience of seeing that whenever he says *red*, the red cup is lifted up. If a child persists in saying *red* even after the red cup has been lifted up repeatedly, he will discover that *red* does not work as a way of referring to objects of other colors. At that point, the adult player can offer the necessary color term (e.g., *Do you mean blue? The blue one? Do you want me to look under the blue one? Blue?*).

The child's comprehension of color terms is developed when the adult player is the speaker. The adult who guesses *blue* may insist that the child look under the appropriate place (e.g., *I guessed blue. Look under the blue one, not the red one.*). The adult may, in other words, appropriately insist that his or her guess be attended to correctly. This may be accomplished straightforwardly and gently. The adult acts exactly as if someone had passed the pepper instead of the salt he or she requested (*I've already had the pepper. Could I have the salt?*): *I've already guessed red. Would you look under the blue now?* As the child comes to comprehend and produce two color terms, one new color may be introduced.

Two-Word Versions (Level II-A)

This format may be used in games designed to elicit two-word utterances. To create a two-word game, it is necessary to use large objects that may be differentiated only by using more than one word. For example, one might use a big doll, a small doll, a big teddy bear, and a small teddy bear. To pick out any one of these toys, it is necessary to say whether the toy is big or small *and* whether it is a doll or a teddy bear. Color terms may be used as modifiers in two-term games. For example, the objects may be a red truck, a blue truck, a red hat, and a blue hat.

When beginning to play games that call for modifier-noun combinations, children usually provide only one of the two terms necessary. For instance, if the materials consist of red and blue hats and trucks, the child is apt to say only *red, blue, truck,* or *hat.* In that case, the adult simply says: "Which one?" The adult may also model the possible forms by saying, "The red truck?", "The red hat?", and so forth. Usually, the child begins to produce strings of single-word utterances (e.g., *red,* then *hat*). Eventually, these strings of single words emerge as two-word, modifier-noun combinations.

The materials required for these games are bulky. It is also difficult to locate objects that are similar in all ways except the dimension of interest, such as color and size. Consequently, two-word games are generally easier to manage and construct using pictures. If a child lacks matching skills and does not understand pictorial representation, word combinations may be taught using these two-word games. In most instances, however, it is easier to use other formats.

Hiding Games with Pictures

Hiding Games with Pictures are appropriate for many purposes with children of varied abilities. Instead of hiding a small object under one of a set of large objects, the listener hides a small object (e.g., a coin or poker chip) or picture under one of a set of pictures. To guess where the small object or picture is hidden, the speaker must describe pictures in the set.

These Hiding Games may be played with drawings, commercially available photographs, or photographs taken specifically for the games. A particular advantage of the Hiding Game format is that these games do not require duplicate sets of pictures as do, for example, Lotto Games. Consequently, a set of pictures that appeals to a child may be used in a Hiding Game without the time and expense of duplication. Pictures taken during a field trip may be used in a Hiding Game immediately after the field trip. Family photographs, pictures from magazines, and other materials may be put to use immediately and easily in these games.

The main disadvantage of this format, as opposed to those discussed in later chapters, is that it does not provide the kind of clear, redundant feedback that is available in Lotto, Bingo, Picture-Toy, and Identical Arrangement formats. The child who lacks matching skills is, however, unable to use feedback that comes from the observation of a match, so this is not a serious drawback for those children.

The master game in this series is used to teach the names of classmates. Other games may be used to build vocabulary, including specialized kinds of vocabulary; to teach the use of modifiers, locatives, and meaningful counting; and to teach the production and comprehension of various multiterm constructions.

Prerequisites

This format requires picture recognition skills but not matching skills. Consequently, it is particularly useful for children who lack the latter. It does, however, appeal to some children who have well-developed matching skills; many children simply like this format.

Note that label elicitation activities are not appropriate checks on the picture recognition skills needed for these games. A child may recognize the people or objects shown in pictures yet be unable to label them. The adult who uses a label elicitation activity does not find out whether the child who fails to provide the label does not recognize the correspondence between the person or object and the picture or sees the correspondence but does not supply the label.

For children who have difficulty with picture recognition, the use of an instant camera is sometimes helpful. The adult photographs the relevant person or object, and the child immediately watches the image appear in the photograph. Whether the pictures used are instant or not, the child's recognition may be checked by asking the child to go to or point to the person or object depicted.

Players

These games may be played by dyads or fairly large groups. The only restriction on group size is that all participants must be able to see all of the pictures.

The People in Our Class (Level I-B)

This game helps children learn the names of their classmates and teachers. A small picture, piece of paper, or other small, flat object is hidden under one of a set of photographs, and the speaker guesses where the object is hidden by naming the people in the pictures.

Materials
The game requires a photograph of each of the people whose names the child is to learn. Each photograph should show only one person. The photographs must be recognizable ones, not blurred snapshots or photographs showing uncharacteristic expressions. In initial playing, it is helpful to include pictures of children and adults who are particular favorites of the child.

How to Play
For a child functioning at a very low cognitive level, two pictures are used. The speaker closes his eyes while the listener hides the poker chip, piece of paper, or other small object under one of the photographs. When the object is hidden, the speaker is told to open his eyes and to guess where the object is. The adult may initially provide repeated models of responses (e.g., *Billy? Mary? The picture of Mary? Billy?*). If a child seems unable to produce a response, it may be helpful to rephrase the question as a yes-no question (*Is it under Mary's picture?*). If this is done, a yes or no response should be accepted. As soon as the child produces any reponse that may be interpreted as a choice of one of the pictures, the listener lifts the picture to see whether the object is there. If it is not, the adult provides the child with appropriate praise for having guessed (*Good guess. Not there. Let's try again.*). Failure to find the object on the first try is not discouraging or negatively reinforcing, since the failure of the guess prolongs the play (*You get another turn to guess.*). The child is then encouraged to guess again until the object is located. If multiple players are involved, they take turns as speakers.

One-Picture Version (Level I-B)
A very simple version of this game uses only one picture. This version is suitable for a child who speaks very little and perhaps recognizes only a few

photographs. When playing the one-picture version, any vocal response the child makes may be interpreted as an instruction to lift up the picture and search for the object.

Vocabulary-Building Versions (Level I-B)

Simple Hiding Games may be used to teach basic vocabulary. Hiding Games may be played with pictures of animals, vehicles, places in the classroom, superheroes — virtually anything that can be shown clearly in a photograph or drawing.

Nouns are relatively easy to depict in this way. For example, one can teach nouns related to Halloween by playing a Hiding Game with pictures of pumpkins, witches, and masks. When a game has a particular theme (Halloween, Christmas, animals, etc.), it is enjoyable to use a small picture related to the same theme as the object to be hidden. For instance, a small picture of a witch can be the hidden object, and the children can guess where the witch is hiding — under the picture of the pumpkin or the mask. A similar game for Christmas consists of finding Santa Claus.

Colors may be taught if the object is hidden under cards that differ in color. Other modifiers may be taught as well. For example, a Halloween game can show two different pumpkins, one smiling and one frowning (crying). Note that if one wants to teach modifiers alone and not two-word combinations, it is important that the objects be as identical as possible so that the modifier is required to differentiate between the pictures. In the above example, *pumpkin* or *jack-o'-lantern* does not convey the information needed to play the game: There is a reason to use a modifier. Unless the speaker says which pumpkin is meant, the listener cannot tell whether the speaker means the smiling pumpkin or the frowning one.

Hiding Games with Pictures may also be used to teach locatives, using, for example, commercially available sets of cards intended to teach prepositions. A set of cards showing the same cat under a box, on top of a box, and next to a box is suitable. To differentiate among these pictures, it is necessary to specify the location of the cat. Describing either the agent (the cat) or the object of the preposition (the box) does not work, since all of the pictures show the cat and the box.

Quantifiers, including numbers, may also be taught in this format. A set of pictures may show one cat, two cats, and three cats. To specify which picture should be lifted up, the speaker needs to use the words *one*, *two*, and *three*. This production of number words occurs in a meaningful context. The child who says *two* to instruct the listener to search under the picture of two cats uses the word *two* to refer to two objects and to issue a command. In practice, the speaker often replies "two" after having been asked the question, "How many cats?''. The response, *two*, then, is a meaningful one and is not the kind of meaningless recitation involved in rattling off *one, two, three, four, five*.

Two-Word Hiding Games (Level II-A)

Hiding Games may be used to elicit various two-word constructions, including agent-object, agent-action, modifier-noun, agent-location, and others. Commercially available photographs virtually never meet the requirements for two-word games. These games must generally be constructed from photographs taken specifically for them.

The materials for a two-word Hiding Game often consist of four pictures. For example, two pictures may show one person or object, while two show another. Two of the pictures must show one action, modifier, or location; and two of the pictures show another. For example, a set of four pictures suitable for two-word Hiding Games might include a dog eating ice cream, the same dog drinking milk, a cat eating ice cream, and the same cat drinking milk. The containers for the milk and ice cream should be visible. To take a photograph, choose a carton of ice cream with a picture of a dish of ice cream on it. Put it next to the dish containing the food. Let the animal loose on the food, then quickly snap the picture.

Another set of four pictures might consist of one cat, two cats, one dog, and two dogs. This game can be constructed using stickers. Put the required number of stickers on each of four 3 by 5 cards, then laminate the cards. Four more pictures — Child A on the chair, Child A under the chair, Child B on the chair, and Child B under the chair — can be created by photographing each child on, then under the same chair. One final example is to have pictures showing Child A playing with Playdough, Child A at the water table, Child B playing with Playdough, and Child B at the water table. To create these, photograph the children as they engage in school activities. Be careful to include only the target child in each picture.

In each of the above examples, one word alone will not pick out a particular picture. In the final example, for instance, *Playdough* does not tell the listener which child is using Playdough, while a name does not tell whether the child is using Playdough or playing at the water table. As discussed above, when children first play these two-word games, they initially produce only one of the required two pieces of information. The use of these materials does not result in the immediate production of two-word constructions. The child first communicates the two pieces of information separately, then communicates the two pieces of information in a single construction.

Two-word Hiding Games may use more than four pictures if the number of people, objects, activities, or locations is expanded. For instance, if one is working with a group of three children, one might photograph each of the children performing two different actions, yielding a set of six pictures.

Simple two-word Hiding Games may also be played with a set of three pictures, only two of which must be described using two words. For example, a set of pictures for such a game might show Child A on a swing, Child B on a swing, and Child B and a slide. In this case, the use of Child A's name refers unambiguously to the first picture. The inclusion of "easy" items like this in a rather demanding game provides children with a chance to experience successful communication. This interjection of simple elements into relatively complex games seems to help children make transitions to difficult games without experiencing them as simply one more context in which to fail at language.

Three-Word Hiding Games (Level III-A)

Three-word Hiding Games use the same principles as two-word games. For example, two children can be photographed separately doing two things in two separate places (e.g., Child A sitting on a chair, sitting on the floor, standing on a chair, and standing on the floor, with analogous pictures of Child B).

In practice, it is often convenient to create a three-word game with a less-than-complete set. Some activities, for example, are unlikely to occur in certain locations. When photographing animals or objects, the materials necessary for a "perfect" game may not be available. The important point is to use a few pictures requiring three-word descriptions. The children will not be distressed if all pictures fail to require three-word descriptions. For example, three pictures in a favorite game among the children with whom we work show one cat drinking milk, eating ice cream, and eating crackers. The remaining pictures in the game show two cats, then a dog performing the same activities. The pictures involving two cats could, in fact, be described using two words (e.g., *two*, *crackers*), although children seldom offer such descriptions. This kind of incomplete or imperfect set of pictures is pedagogically effective, if logically incomplete.

Complex Hiding Games: Warnings

Once one grasps the idea of creating sets of materials in which any one picture requires an elaborate description to be designated unambiguously, it is all too easy to create games that are excessively demanding. For example, a trial Halloween game involving a set of pictures of witches proved to be rather demanding for adults (e.g., *The old witch wearing a hat is stirring a pot, and green bubbles are coming out of the pot, and there are bats flying around in the background* was too elaborate a description to expect.).

Once one begins to play multiword games, it is also tempting to ask children to say more than is communicatively required. For example, in a game described previously, if a child says, "Two cat eat ice cream," one may feel compelled to ask the child to say, *Two cats are eating ice cream.* The addition of the *-s* and the auxiliary *are* is not communicatively necessary and should not be required. One may, however, model the adult form (*Let's see, you said, "Two cats are eating ice cream!"*). In some cases one may also, as the speaker in the game, use the adult form (e.g., *the cats* rather than *two cats*) in such a way that the child must decode that form. Repetition of the child's meaning in expanded form can and should be done frequently. When the adult players speak, they speak ordinarily, using articles, auxiliaries, and other forms that the children omit. This kind of modeling is sufficient, and an arbitrary insistence that children use the elaborate trimmings of language is counterproductive.

Articulation Hiding Games

The Hiding Game format may be used for work on articulation if the pictures require the production of specified sounds. For example, a minimal-pair Hiding Game uses a series of pictures showing a pie, a pipe, a cat, a hat, a bear, a pear, and so forth. If the speaker is to succeed in telling the listener whether to look under the picture of the bear or the pear, for example, the speaker must make the "b"/"p" distinction clear.

Children with relatively advanced cognitive skills readily accept the idea that, in this game, the words are supposed to rhyme or sound alike. They are able to play this as a word game and to agree to use the words that sound alike in this context: *bear* and *pear* rather than, say, *animal* and *fruit*.

Children who do not grasp the convention of using the words that sound alike are nevertheless helped to manage their articulation difficulties. Specifically, the game creates a situation in which they can find ways to circumvent their difficulties in pronouncing words by finding alternative ways to convey their meanings. The search for alternatives can be a source of advancement in syntactic skills. If one is to avoid having to make the "b"/"p" distinction, one often needs to combine words to convey an alternative. English provides no ready synonym for *bear*, and a young child is apt to find that a multiword construction is the easiest way to avoid the difficult phonological distinction. For example, *he got fur* or *eat it* may represent alternatives to *bear* and *pear* that stretch the child's ability to use verbs or combine words.

Narrative Hiding Games

In Narrative Hiding Games, a character searches for something in a series of probable places. For example, the Cookie Monster looks for a cookie in an oven, a refrigerator, a cookie jar, and a cupboard. A father lion looks for his baby by seeing whether the baby is visiting various other animals in the jungle.

Materials

The "protagonist" in the story is a hand puppet, such as the Cookie Monster. The hidden object is something the protagonist would want, such as a cookie. The places the protagonist looks are marked by pictures fastened to disposable plastic cups.

How to Play

The speaker puts on the hand puppet and closes his eyes. The listener hides the object under one of the up-ended cups. The speaker then has the puppet guess where the object is, while the listener checks out the guess.

The adult may narrate this process. When introducing the game, the adult may begin a story: *Cookie Monster knew there was a cookie hidden someplace in the kitchen. He wanted to find it.* The adult may also provide a narrative as the child guesses. Finally, the adult may provide a conclusion: *At last, the Cookie Monster found the cookie in the oven, and he ate the cookie all up.* The child with the puppet may celebrate the finding of the cookie by having the Cookie Monster "eat" the cookie.

If the lost object is a baby animal, the conclusion of the story may be that the father lion gives the baby a big hug; similarly, that Miss Piggy finally finds her mirror and takes a long look at herself; or another appropriate ending.

A Note on the Rules

Hiding Games, like all communication games, have only one basic rule: Use words. In Hiding Games, this rule means that the children must use words to guess where the object is hidden. They must not grab the large objects or pictures. This rule should be enforced.

Another frequent violation of the rules may safely be ignored: Young children often peek when they are supposed to be closing their eyes. If one is playing with a relatively advanced and socially skilled group of children, this behavior is quickly censured by the group (*Jason's peeking. Jason, you're peeking.*). If this kind of group pressure occurs, one helps the offending child to adapt to the demand from the group. Otherwise, peeking does not interfere with the game. In fact, the child who peeks knows exactly what he should guess and has a strong motivation to describe the picture or large object where he knows the small object is hidden. Peeking, then, is not an important violation of the rules of the game.

Adult peeking may also be helpful. It is generally necessary when playing with a very immature child to keep one's eye on the child all the time. The child who may run away, destroy pictures, or otherwise engage in undesirable behavior needs to be watched, and a rigid adherence to the no-peeking rule would involve leaving the child unattended. A child just learning to play Hiding Games generally has some trouble informing the adult listener that it is time to look. Consequently, one must monitor the child's behavior. In other words, peek. It may be helpful to remind the child during the time that one has one's eyes covered that he should be doing certain things (e.g., *Remember, put the picture on top of the chip.*). It may also be necessary to prompt the child to tell you to look (e.g., *Can I look now? Ready? Tell me when you're ready. Ready?*). Unless the adult peeks, these prompts and reminders cannot be timed correctly.

When playing with a relatively skilled child who does not require constant monitoring, the adult may abide by the no-peeking rule. In that case, the adult really does not know where the child has hidden the object. The adult really guesses. This genuineness contributes a lively quality to the playing; when all players actually are guessing, the interaction has a special quality it may lack if the adult secretly knows the right answer.

Perceptive Players

A perceptive child experienced at playing Hiding Games learns to scan an array of pictures for physical clues about the location of the hidden object. A poker chip or coin is a giveaway for such a child. If the child's immediate recognition of the hiding place spoils the game, a small piece of paper or picture should be used as the hidden object.

Summary

Hiding Games are simple guessing games in which the listener hides a small object and the speaker guesses its location. In the Hiding Games with Objects, the small object is hidden in a player's hands, under a larger object, or in another place, but not under drawings or photographs. Hiding Games with Objects require neither picture recognition nor matching skills and are useful with children functioning at low cognitive and linguistic levels. This format is useful to teach proper names, nouns, and modifiers, including color terms. It may be used to teach some two-term constructions, but other formats are more appropriate for that purpose.

In Hiding Games with Pictures, the listener hides a small, flat object under one of a series of pictures, and the speaker guesses the location of the hidden object. These games require picture recognition but not picture matching skills. This format may be used to teach nouns, modifiers, quantifiers, locatives, verbs, two-term constructions, three-term constructions, and articulation. Although uniquely appropriate for children who lack matching skills, Hiding Games are useful in many other instances as well.

6

Communicative Lotto and Bingo

Lotto and Bingo Games are probably familiar to all adults. A caller holds a deck of picture cards or draws tokens with numbers written on them. The caller displays and calls out one picture or number (e.g., the familiar *B6*, *N9*, etc. from Bingo). Each player has a card showing pictures or numbers. The player who has the picture or number displayed by the caller covers the appropriate picture or number on his card. The first player to fill a card (or column) by covering all the pictures or numbers wins.

As Lotto Games are usually played in preschools, they do not require the use of language. The caller holds a set of pictures and simply displays one picture. The player whose card shows that picture claims it and places it over the matching picture on his card. Played in this manner, Lotto is a matching game and does not involve language. In an effort to make Lotto a language game, teachers sometimes require that the caller call out the picture in addition to displaying it. For example, instead of merely holding up a picture of a zebra, a child may be asked to say *Who has the zebra?* while displaying the picture. The players may also be required to respond verbally to claim the card (e.g., *I do.* or *I have the zebra.*). Because the caller displays the card, however, there is no real need to talk in this kind of Lotto. The requirement that the children call out the cards and claim them with words is arbitrary.

With a slight change in the rules, Lotto becomes a communication game.

Instead of being asked to display the card, the caller is forbidden to do so. Rather, he must describe the picture without showing it. When this rule is invoked, the caller or speaker has information to communicate that is not transmitted visually. The listener or listeners need to understand the caller's words to play.

Communicative Lotto teaches vocabulary, syntax, and articulation. Unlike the Hiding Games discussed previously, Lotto Games require picture recognition and matching skills. Furthermore, the format of Lotto Games is somewhat more difficult for very young children and for children functioning at low cognitive levels than the Hiding Game format. In general, there is no need to complicate the game by introducing the competitive element that makes Bingo or Beano a game for adults. Children are usually happy to play simply to keep playing; some children, however, enjoy playing to win.

The main advantage of Lotto and Bingo over the simpler Hiding Games is that the use of duplicate materials permits children to verify their referential communication by looking at the materials. If an adult says "cat" and the child selects the picture of a cat, the adult then shows the child a picture identical to the one he selected. The match or mismatch of pictures provides feedback about the adequacy of communication — feedback that comes from the materials, not simply from adult judgments.

Bingo versus Lotto

The difference between Lotto and Bingo lies mainly in what is used to cover up the items on the cards. In Lotto, a picture is claimed from the caller and used to cover the corresponding picture on the card. In Bingo, an arbitrary marker, such as a poker chip, is used. Consequently, in Bingo, a picture may appear more than once. The advantage of Bingo, using chips rather than pictures, is that several different players may respond to the same picture. When the dealer says "zebra," several different players may respond, covering the zebras on their cards. In Lotto, however, each picture may occur on only one playing card, since only one player may claim the picture. Because the chips are arbitrary markers, some children have difficulty playing Bingo but no trouble with Lotto. If a child seems to find the poker chips confusing one should stay with the simpler Lotto format.

Bingo and Lotto

Because Bingo and Lotto are otherwise identical, they are not discussed separately here. Any game described in the Lotto format may be played in exactly the same way using Bingo materials (chips) instead.

Prerequisite Skills

Lotto Games require picture recognition and matching skills. The child who fails to recognize or match line drawings of a generalized object may perform better with a color photograph of a familiar example of the object. Photographs of familiar people, for example, may be recognizable and matchable when photographs depicting abstractions ("children") are not. If, however, a child simply does not get the idea that two identical pictures are the same, Lotto is not an appropriate format for that child.

Players

Lotto may be played by dyads; one person is the speaker, the other the listener. The object of the game is to have the listener cover up his or her pictures with matching ones.

When there are three or more players, the speaker needs to know which of the listeners has the picture he is describing. The adult speaker may avoid obtaining that information visually by looking fixedly at his or her picture while asking the children, "Who has a...?".

Vocabulary Lotto (Level I-C)

The simplest version of Lotto helps children to build vocabulary. The game may be used to teach the names of animals, people, silverware, color terms, locatives, numbers, or virtually any other single-word element that can be shown pictorially.

Materials

Two identical sets of pictures are required. Commercially available Lotto games have one set of small pictures and one set of Lotto cards, each showing six or eight of the smaller pictures. The use of large Lotto cards has some disadvantages for the communication games. It is sometimes preferable to be able to select the number of pictures from which a child chooses or to add or delete pictures. Consequently, instead of using Lotto cards, the adult selects the desired pictures and arrays them in front of the child.

Some commercially available Lotto games use drawings that pose challenges of interpretation. While the animal Lotto Games are fairly easy to interpret, games showing "familiar" places and objects are often very difficult for children to interpret. Instead of using commercial Lotto Games, one may construct Lotto Games using photographs or sets of stickers. There are several points to bear in mind when constructing Lotto games. These points, and some specific suggestions for Lotto games, appear in chapter 12.

How to Play

The adult selects two small sets of identical pictures, such as a set of three clear photographs of children in the child's class and a duplicate set of those photographs. One set is placed in front of the child. (*Always* place pictures so they are right side up from the child's viewpoint.) The other set is placed face down in a pile. The adult lifts up the top picture. He or she does not show it to the child, but tells the child which person is shown in the picture (e.g., *I have the picture of Mary.*). The adult instructs the child to point to the picture of the person named. As soon as the child places a finger on one of the pictures, the child is shown the picture the adult is holding. The adult and child compare the pictures to see whether they match (*Are they the same?*). If the pictures are identical, the adult's picture is given to the child, who uses it to cover the identical one in his array. The adult then draws another picture, and the process is repeated until the cards are used up.

If the child has placed his finger on the wrong picture, the adult simply points out the mismatch (e.g., *Whoops, they aren't the same. This is Mary, but this one is Billy. Let's try again.*). The adult may then repeat the process with the same picture. When a match occurs, the adult congratulates the child, exclaims about the match, and otherwise rewards the child for understanding accurately. When a mismatch occurs, the adult simply points out that things went wrong this time, but does not criticize the child. (If many mismatches occur, the child is not ready for the particular game.)

Once the child has covered all of his sets of pictures with the duplicates, the roles in the game reverse. The child becomes the speaker. While in the role of listener, the adult asks for clarification when the child is unclear. If the adult cannot understand what the child says, he or she asks for repetitions and clarifications (*I can't hear you.* or *Tell me again.*). When children first assume the role of caller, they almost invariably do one of two things: They display the picture instead of describing it, or they reach over and point out the picture to which the adult should point. The adult simply reminds the child of the rules, generally by pointing out that the adult did not show the picture or point (*Remember, no showing the picture. I didn't show you, did I?*).

Competitive Versions

Lotto and Bingo may, of course, be played competitively: The person who covers his or her pictures first wins. The whole idea of winning is foreign to many young special-needs children. To introduce winning would complicate the game and confuse the child. There are, however, instances in which children enjoy playing competitively. First, some children come from families that play competitive games together. An occasional child is used to playing competitively and enjoys this kind of game. Second, nonhandicapped, mainstreamed children sometimes think of games as competitive games. If they play, they want to play competitively or not at all. Competition, then, can be used to induce these children to play. Third, group games involving competition can be motivating for all children. The children in the group who are less able than the others may not be aware of the competitive element at all, but the general sense of excitement and fun is motivating to them. The competitive element is, however, kept low-key. A skilled adult, too, can easily rig a game so that everyone has a chance to win.

An alternative to outright competition is the invocation of a rule that the first listener to fill his card becomes the speaker in the next round of the game.

The Content of Vocabulary Lotto Games

Bingo or Lotto may be used to teach virtually any content that can be depicted effectively. All of the materials described previously for Hiding Games with Pictures may be used in Lotto and Bingo Games if duplicate sets of pictures are available.

Nouns may be taught simply by photographing appropriate objects and duplicating those photographs. Lotto Games may be used to teach words for the foods served in the children's homes (*milk, eggs, bread, ice cream, pizza, juice*). The games may help children learn words for familiar places in the school and for daily activities (*circle time, snack time, bathroom*). Nouns associated with particular holidays may be taught with Lotto Games made from stickers available seasonally (*Santa Claus, Christmas tree, stocking, pumpkin, witch, ghost*).

Modifiers may also be taught in this format rather than in the Hiding Game format. Color Lotto Games may be purchased, but it is easy to construct them. (Be sure to use only clear, bright, unambiguous colors. Origami paper works well.) Commercially available color Lotto Games are sometimes too difficult for special-needs children, mainly because the large cards usually show too many colors. If one cuts up the cards from those games or makes cards showing only two or three colors, the game is easier.

Some commercially available sets of "language" materials can be used to create communicative Lotto Games if one orders duplicate sets. For example, "Positions" cards are useful in teaching locatives (e.g., the cat is in the box, the cat is on the box, etc.). Sets of cards designed to teach numbers may also be purchased in duplicate and used in Lotto Games (e.g., two identical sets of cards showing one cat, two cats, and three cats).

Commercially available materials are sometimes less satisfactory when one wants to teach verbs than when one wants to teach nouns or modifiers. Depictions of jumping, hopping, and so forth are seldom as clear as one needs. Pictures of the children themselves performing actions are sometimes effective. For example, a Lotto Game can be created by photographing a child sitting, standing, swinging, touching his toes, and so forth; these photographs must be duplicated for use in Lotto.

Two-Word Versions (Level II-A)

Two-word Lotto Games may be played with the same pictures used in two-word Hiding Games, but the pictures must be duplicated. The same general principle is involved in constructing these games: Two pieces of information are necessary to refer unambiguously to any one picture. A useful device in designing two-word games is a 2 by 2 table, as shown in Figure 1.

The second table in Figure 1 illustrates one of the difficulties of making two-word games: taking the pictures one might like. Blue and red planes must be photographs of toy planes, and those planes should differ only in color. Furthermore, each plane should be only one color. The necessary toys are not always readily available.

Multiword Lotto Games (Level III-A)

Multiword Lotto Games may be created by combining dimensions from the easier one- and two-word versions. For example, numbers, colors, and objects may be crossed to yield one, two, and three red trucks; one, two, and three blue trucks; and one, two, and three blue cars. Note that a perfect, complete matrix arrangement is not absolutely necessary; some interesting content simply will not fit into ideal designs. For example, agent-action-object constructions (e.g., *The girl is holding the cat.*) are sometimes impossible or unlikely if the roles of the nouns are reversed to teach contrastive word order (e.g., *The cat is holding the girl.*). The important point is to include at least one pair of pictures that requires a three-word construction, not to insist on perfection.

Articulation Lotto

Lotto Games can be designed so that clear articulation is necessary to differentiate among various pictures. As in articulation Hiding Games (chapter 6), the pictures in the game must differ in a single sound. The resulting set shows various minimal pairs: pie/pipe, cap/cat, cat/hat, bell/belt. In both Lotto and Hiding Games, articulation is not taught as an end in itself. Rather, children are able to perceive the need for articulation: If they do not articulate correctly, their listeners misunderstand them.

Puzzle Train Lotto

In this twist on Lotto, the large Lotto cards are puzzle frames depicting trains, with the separate carriages replacing the usual Lotto pictures. It is best played as "double Lotto," so that each player has both a Lotto card and the small matching pictures.

Figure 1
Two-Word Versions

Noun

		Billy	Jason
Verb	run	Billy running	Jason running
	sit	Billy sitting	Jason sitting

Noun

		plane	truck
Modifier	red	red plane	red truck
	blue	blue plane	blue truck

Materials
The Lotto cards are long, narrow puzzle frames (about 15 inches by 4 inches).
Each shows a train with five carriages; each carriage is a different color. The
center of each carriage is a rectangular puzzle piece. When the pieces are
removed, the colored outline of the carriages remains. The puzzle pieces serve
the function of the small matching cards in other Lotto Games.

How to Play
Both players are given puzzle frames, and each is given the pieces that fit in the
other's frames. The object of the game is to have both players complete their
trains.

The speaker begins by asking the listener for one of the needed colors (e.g.,
blue). The listener supplies the puzzle piece, and the speaker fits the piece into
the matching carriage in his puzzle frame. (Obviously, this step involves
feedback.) The listener then becomes the speaker and requests a color needed
for his train.

The game can be played in this way until each player's train is complete. In
this case, the content the game teaches is simply the use of color terms as
single-word utterances. Its advantage is that it provides an opportunity to
teach conjunctions, negation, and other linguistic devices as a means of
referring to classes or subclasses of colors. Specifically, each player may take
his first turn as speaker by saying something like: *Give me any color.* A
player's second turn as speaker may involve saying: *Any color but blue*, and
the third, *Anything except blue or red* or *Not blue and not red.* The final turn
may be: *I need the only one you have left.*

While children may play effectively without producing these kinds of
utterances, the adult may use them, providing a model and helping children
comprehend them in the meaningful context of the game.

Because of the somewhat complicated nature of the game — each player's
pieces fit in someone else's puzzle — it is best mastered as a two-person game
before other players are introduced. Adept players, however, may play with as
many participants as there are puzzle frames: Each player has the pieces that fit
the puzzle of one other player.

Lotto Card Arrays

In some Lotto Games and in Hiding Games with Pictures, the adult must
select a set of pictures equivalent to the master card in conventional Lotto and
Bingo. As noted previously, the use of arrays of pictures instead of master cards
with a fixed set of pictures is advantageous. The adult may add and delete
pictures in seconds. This advantage, however, places a burden on the adult to

exercise judgment in the choice of sets. How many pictures should be presented to a child? Which pictures?

Commercially available Lotto and Bingo Games usually have master cards containing a relatively large number of pictures, as many as 16 or 25 in games like color Bingo. In games for special-needs children, the optimum number of pictures depends on the child and the content of the game. A Hiding Game for a child functioning at a very low linguistic level may be played with a single picture. Hiding and Lotto may be played using arrays of only two pictures. The advantage of arrays, in contrast to master cards, is that a child may begin playing with only a few pictures. One new picture may then be added. Another new one may be added in the next round of the game. If the game becomes too difficult for the child, a picture may be deleted in the next round.

When introducing a child to a new set of Lotto or Hiding Game materials, it is generally best to begin with quick rounds of games, using only a few pictures. The pictures are selected so that the games require only one-word utterances. Thus, the child learns the basic vocabulary needed to comprehend and produce word combinations in later rounds. For example, suppose that the following set of photographs is available in duplicate for use in Lotto:

1. a girl on a swing
2. the girl on a slide
3. the girl in a sandbox
4. a boy on a swing
5. the boy on a slide
6. the boy in a sandbox

The first rounds of the game might be played with only two pictures showing one child in two different places, that is, pictures 1 and 2, 1 and 3, 2 and 3, 4 and 5, 4 and 6, or 5 and 6. Subsequent rounds might be played using another of these subsets of two pictures. The purpose of games using these subsets of pictures is to teach the comprehension and production of locative terms needed to describe where the actors are in the picture.

When selecting the new subsets, it is a good idea to include one picture with which the child has already worked. For example, if the child has played the game using pictures 1 and 2, another round might be played using 1 and 3. In this case, the child could use his knowledge of picture 1 (the girl in the swing) to learn to talk about picture 3.

Other subsets of pictures would be used to teach the terms to describe the children in the pictures. In those subsets, the location would remain constant, while the actor was varied. These subsets would consist of pictures 1 and 4, 2 and 5, and 3 and 6.

The number of pictures in an array might then be increased without raising the level of the game. Specifically, pictures 1, 2, and 3 might be used in one array; pictures 4, 5, and 6 would be used in another array. In any one round of the game, then, the child would need to produce only one-word utterances, but the number of pictures in the array would be increased.

The next step would be to select a subset of the three pictures for which a one-term description would be ambiguous. For example, pictures 1, 2, and 4 would be such a subset. Additional pictures could then be added so that the child would begin to work with larger arrays. Eventually, all six pictures in the set could be used simultaneously in one round of the game.

The speed with which the process of moving from one-word, two-picture arrays to two-term, six-picture arrays can take place depends on the child. The general guide for deciding how many pictures to use, then, is to begin with a small number and to add pictures gradually so that a child learns new terms in contrast with familiar ones. If a child has been working with a set of two pictures, a third is added. When the child masters that, a fourth is added.

"Rifflers"

An occasional child disrupts the smooth flow of play by repeatedly shuffling, picking up, fingering, and otherwise manipulating the pictures. There are several ways to handle this "riffling."

First, children sometimes enjoy simply looking at pictures without playing games with them. In this case, the child's bothersome riffling of the pictures during the game may tell the adult that the child needs a chance to treat the pictures as ordinary snapshots. The adult and child may look through the pictures, talk about them, and otherwise satisfy the child's urge to take a good, relaxed look.

Second, if the child's behavior indicates some anxiety about the game, the adult may change the child's program in some way, as discussed in chapter 3.

Third, riffling may be a part of a child's general restlessness. Faced with a bunch of objects, the child may be unable to control an urge to grab. A set of pictures neatly arrayed before a listener in Lotto is less tantalizing than a pile of pictures. When such a child is the speaker in Lotto, the adult may need to retain control of the deck of speaker's cards. The adult holds the deck face down and presents it to the child; the adult instructs the child to take the top card or to take one card.

Summary

Communicative Lotto and Bingo differ from conventional versions of these games. Instead of displaying the calling card, the speaker conceals the calling card and transmits the information shown on the card by talking. The listener uses the information the speaker transmits to select one of the pictures on a master card. The speaker then displays the calling card, and the players compare the calling card with the listener's selection. In comparing the two pictures, the players receive feedback about the effectiveness or ineffectiveness of the communication.

Bingo and Lotto require picture recognition and picture matching skills. These games may be used to teach vocabulary, and they provide a structured context for teaching the meaningful use of two-term and multiterm constructions. They may also be used to work on articulation errors that affect meaning.

7
Picture-Toy
Matching Games

The materials for Picture-Toy Matching Games are sets of toys with corresponding sets of photographs or other pictures of those toys. The speaker uses the pictures to direct the listener's manipulation of the toys. Because these games involve toys, they are very appealing to children. As pedagogical devices, they have other advantages as well. The speaker has the opportunity to direct the listener's actions. Because the speaker can see what the listener is doing, he or she can provide corrective feedback. The listener, who is manipulating the toys, often needs to request clarification. These games, then, foster an interchange between players and encourage the use of language to direct others, to request information, and to provide clarification.

Picture-Toy Matching Games can be simple, one-word games. A particular advantage of this format, however, is that it lends itself to the creation of complex, highly motivating games using coordinated sets of interesting materials. For example, this format is used for games involving large toy farms, zoos, villages, and other complicated arrays of toys. Most classrooms contain sets of toys that can be photographed for use in Picture-Toy Matching Games.

Picture-Toy Matching Games

Players

The players may be one adult and one child, or two children supervised by an adult bystander. If active roles are provided to all children, the adult may sometimes contrive to include three children in games played in this format. It is, however, absolutely essential that no child be required to wait passively while others play. In particular, the adult must not play several rounds of a game with one child while another child simply sits and waits until it is his or her turn to play with the adult. The adult who must work with two or more children should forfeit his or her own central role rather than force a child into the bystander role.

Prerequisites

The children must recognize the photographs as representative of the toys; they must also recognize a match or mismatch between the arrangements of toys depicted in the photographs and the actual arrangements of the toys. Finally, the children must be able to manipulate the toys to achieve the arrangements depicted.

A warm-up period is sometimes helpful to check and reinforce the prerequisite skills: The children practice using the photographs as guides to select and arrange toys, without trying to communicate with others about the materials.

The Family (Level I-C)

This game helps children learn family names (*mommy, daddy, baby, girl, boy*). A slightly more complex version involves using words for the actions of these characters (e.g., *The mommy is sitting; the daddy is standing.*).

Materials

The materials required are a set of dolls showing a family: a mother, father, and several children. The dolls should be large enough for the children to manipulate easily. If possible, the dolls should be poseable; in particular, they should be able to sit and stand (if propped against something). In addition to the dolls, one piece of toy furniture is needed — a chair, bed, or simply a block on which a doll may sit and that can be used to prop up a doll while it stands. Finally, the game requires a set of photographs of the dolls in the same position and location. For example, a set may show:

- the mother sitting on a chair
- the father sitting on a chair
- the baby sitting on a chair
- the girl sitting on a chair

How to Play

The adult places the set of photographs face down on the playing surface. The listener is given the toys. The speaker selects one picture and describes that picture without showing it to the listener (e.g., *The mommy sitting.*). When the listener does something with the toys, the speaker shows the picture to the listener. The adult and the child or children check to see whether the selection of the doll matches that shown in the photograph. If the listener's selection is correct, the adult verbally points out the match between the photograph and the toys (e.g., *Yes, here is the mommy, and here is the mommy. It looks just like the picture.*). The players then switch roles.

Theme Games (Levels II-A and III-A)

Theme games are games about a zoo, a farm, a village, a set of superheroes, or another appealing theme. Although a full set of toys and pictures for a theme game contains many toys and pictures, children begin playing these games with a selected subset of materials. Once a child is adept at playing with a few subsets, these may be combined so that the set of materials used gradually becomes larger and larger.

There are two particular caveats about the use of theme games. First, the games are attractive and may be overwhelmingly so: A child suddenly presented with a whole set of toys may become overstimulated. Second, children sometimes take rather a long time to arrange the toys in these games. A child who takes a long time may slow the pace of the game so that it becomes tedious for other children. Consequently, children should be introduced to these games gradually so that they are not overwhelmed. Furthermore, a child should first play with an adult alone; the child who takes a long time to take his turn should not be allowed to prolong the game in a group.

The Zoo

The materials used in the zoo game depict a series of cages, a series of characters visiting the zoo, a series of zoo animals, and several landmarks. The plastic cartons with "bars" used to pack strawberries and other small fruits and vegetables make good cages. The characters may be small dolls or peg dolls. One version uses *Sesame Street* peg dolls (Big Bird and the Cookie Monster) and a peg doll zookeeper who rides in a little car. The landmarks may be bridges, trees, towers, or other objects likely to be found in a zoo. Plastic plants sold in pet supply stores for use in fish tanks make effective and appealing trees. It is important to choose contrasting toys to avoid including both a lion and a tiger or two dolls that look alike. Photographs should be planned carefully so that they form coordinated sets. The following are some suggestions:

- the zebra inside his cage
- the zebra on top of his cage
- the zebra in front of his cage
- the lion inside his cage
- the lion on top of his cage
- the zebra in his cage with Big Bird looking at him
- the zookeeper standing under a tree
- the zebra in his cage with Big Bird on top of the zebra's cage

Similar sets of photographs using other animals and characters may also be used. The photographs should be clear close-ups. When photographing the toys, it is best to use only the toys needed for a particular picture; distracting background details should be avoided (e.g., if the zebra is shown, the lion should not be visible in the background). Do not feature too many animals, characters, and landmarks: A photograph of four characters standing near the tree, looking at the lion, which is on top of its cage, for instance, is too complex.

Linguistic Content

Theme games like the zoo game are particularly useful in teaching agent-action, agent-object, and agent-locative constructions, and in teaching compounds. Agent-action constructions, for instance, are elicited using a set of pictures like the following:

- the zebra standing up
- the zebra lying down
- the lion standing up
- the lion lying down

Agent-object constructions are elicited by:

- the zookeeper looking at the lion
- the zookeeper looking at the zebra
- Big Bird looking at the lion
- Big Bird looking at the zebra

Opportunities to show agent-locative combinations are multiple. A simple subset of pictures may show one animal in, next to, and on top of its cage. A coordinated subset may show a different animal in, next to, and on top of its cage. Similarly, two different animals or characters may be shown in relation to two different landmarks.

Compound subjects may be elicited if two different characters or animals are shown. For example:

- the lion and the zebra in the cage
- the elephant and the giraffe in the cage

Compound sentences may be elicited as well:

- the lion in his cage with Big Bird looking at him
- the lion in his cage with Cookie Monster looking at him

Color may be taught by photographing the same animal in two cages that differ in color. Numbers may be taught if two identical animals are used; the photographs might show one lion in the cage and two lions in the cage.

Superhero Games (Level I-C, II-A and III-A)

Games featuring superhero characters may, at first, seem contrary to the overall intent of this program, which is to help children learn to use language in a way that is immediately relevant to their practical needs. Superheroes performing unlikely imaginary activities are far removed from the business of asking for food, commenting on events, and otherwise talking about here-and-now needs and activities. They are, however, relevant to children's interests and to children's interactions with peers. The ability to talk with other children about toys and to exchange information while playing is highly useful to young children. While a child will never actually see a superhero riding on a dinosaur and will thus have no pressing need to communicate the event to adults, the child may pretend that this happens and so benefits from being able to convey information to peers about such imaginary events.

The choice of superheroes rather than other fantasy characters is dictated mainly by the general appeal and familiarity of these characters. They are attractive not only to children with language problems but to other children as well. Batman and Superman dolls are a great incentive to all the children in a class to participate in the games. The verbal child who is mainstreamed or who is in a special-needs class because of orthopedic difficulties, emotional problems, or other problems is eager to play with these toys. Unhappily, female superhero dolls seem to be nonexistent. Female characters from *Star Wars* and various other films and television shows are sometimes available but are seldom familiar to the young children with whom we work.

Materials

Two superhero dolls are needed. These are often available in two sizes: one about 6 inches high, the other about 4 inches high. The larger ones are expensive, while the small are inexpensive; consequently, we use the smaller ones. Fisher-Price Adventure People may be used as well.

A set of objects to be used with the dolls is also needed. For example, one set consists of a toy bathtub, a toy refrigerator, and a toy double bunk bed. Another set consists of a toy boat and two different toy dinosaurs. These objects must be in scale with the dolls. They should also be toys that the dolls can "use" in some way. For example, a toy truck that a doll can "drive" is preferable to one in which the doll cannot sit. Toys can sometimes be modified to accommodate the dolls. For example, the cabs of toy trucks can sometimes be cut off so that the dolls can sit in the trucks.

The toys are then photographed in predetermined arrangements. For example, suppose the set of toys consists of Superman, the Incredible Hulk, a toy boat, and a dinosaur. The set of pictures designed to elicit two-word utterances might be as follows (Level II-A):

- Superman riding in the boat
- Superman riding on the dinosaur
- the Hulk riding in the boat
- the Hulk riding on the dinosaur

Another set might show (Level II-A):

- Superman lying down
- Superman standing up
- the Hulk lying down
- the Hulk standing up
- the dinosaur lying down
- the dinosaur standing up

A particular favorite devised by the children with whom we work is as follows (Level III-A):

- the dinosaur biting the Hulk's foot
- the dinosaur biting the Hulk's head
- the dinosaur biting Superman's foot
- the dinosaur biting Superman's head

While this set is very popular among some children, children who are upset about its aggressive content should not be expected to play with it.

When planning the photographs, the most important point is to create one coordinated set. Any of those suggested above is suitable. Two of these may be used at once. For a simple one-word game (Level I-C), only two pictures might be used (e.g., Superman riding on the dinosaur and Superman riding in the boat; the Hulk riding on the dinosaur and Superman riding on the dinosaur). Simple subsets for one-word games can always be extracted from complex sets; simple sets cannot, however, always be combined to form complex sets. Consequently, it is wise to take photographs suitable for complex, two-and three-word games and to use subsets for children who need simple games (see chapter 12).

How to Play

The adult selects one small set of photographs (e.g., Superman riding on the dinosaur and Superman riding in the boat) and gives the listener the toys shown in these photographs. The speaker describes one picture, telling the listener how to arrange the toys (e.g., *Put Superman in the boat. Superman is riding in the boat. Superman is in the boat.*). When the listener has arranged the toys, the speaker shows the photograph to the listener. The two players compare the toys and the photograph. If they match, the adult points out how they match and congratulates the child or children. If they do not match, the adult describes the mismatch and shows the listener how to arrange the toys as they are arranged in the photograph. The listener becomes the speaker and proceeds to describe a picture.

The speaker who uses the photographs can see the listener's arrangement of toys and can give the listener feedback while the toys are being arranged. For example, if the speaker has instructed the listener to put Superman in the boat and the listener starts to put him on the dinosaur, the speaker may say, "Put Superman in the boat, not on the dinosaur. He's not riding on the dinosaur, he's riding in the boat."

Once the child has begun to master one subset of pictures, a different subset may be introduced (e.g, the Hulk riding in the boat and the Hulk riding the dinosaur). When the child begins to master that subset, the two may be combined to make a more difficult game.

Baby and Mommy (Level I-C and II-A)

This game is particularly appropriate for young and developmentally delayed children who have poor fine motor skills. Its content is very appealing to these children, and the toys used are easy to manipulate.

Materials

The toys required are peg dolls, vehicles, and furniture designed for peg dolls. Specifically, the following are needed: one peg doll "baby," one peg doll "woman," one playpen, one stroller, one chair, one rocking horse, one cradle, one truck, and one airplane. A full set of photographs for this game, useful at different levels, might show:

- the baby on the rocking horse
- the baby on the chair
- the baby in the truck
- the baby in the airplane
- the baby lying down in the playpen
- the baby standing up in the playpen
- the baby lying down in the cradle
- the baby standing up outside the playpen
- the mommy on the rocking horse
- the mommy on the chair
- the mommy in the truck
- the mommy in the airplane
- the mommy pushing the baby in the stroller

Other photographs may be useful as well. For example, some children are happy to have the mommy sleep in the cradle, while others resist this improbable position. Children usually reject photographs showing the baby pushing the mommy in the stroller and other improbable role reversals. The improbability of having the baby fly an airplane seems not to bother children and, in fact, was suggested by several children's spontaneous use of the toys in another game format.

How to Play

The speaker uses one photograph to direct the listener's selection and arrangement of the toys. The particular set of photographs from which the speaker selects is determined by the level of the game, as discussed below.

One-Word Versions

This game teaches the simple vocabulary needed to talk about the toys: *baby, mommy, chair, plane,* and so forth. As in other games, it is important not to insist that children use one particular term if another works equally well in the context of the game. For example, the child may refer to the adult doll as *lady,* to the cradle as *bed,* or to the truck as *car.* The adult player, however, may continue to use standard forms and to use those forms in conjunction with the child's own (e.g., *The baby is in the cradle, in the bed.*). A simple and straightforward explanation of terms is sometimes helpful: *A baby's little bed is a cradle. This is a cradle. Sometimes babies sleep in cradles.* An occasional child may call both the cradle and the playpen *bed*. When such ambiguity occurs, the adult listener must, of course, ask for clarification. The simplest way to do so is to point to each possible referent and ask whether the child means the playpen (crib) or the cradle (bed). Any two reasonably accurate terms the child settles on to distinguish between the two pieces of furniture are satisfactory. If the child prefers *crib* and *bed*, *playpen* and *bed*, or another pair, there is no reason to insist that the child say *playpen* and *cradle*.

To use the game to teach one-word utterances, the adult selects sets of photographs in which each photograph may be uniquely identified by means of a single word. For example, the game may be played with only two photographs, each showing a different character in the same place. The result, then, is a game of "Who is riding on the rocking horse?" or "Who is flying the airplane?" In work with any one child, it is a good idea to prepare the child for other versions of this game by using a variety of photographs. For instance, instead of using only the photographs of the two characters riding on the rocking horse, it is a good idea to alternate showing them on the rocking horse, in the plane, and so on. The adult, in describing the various pictures, models sequences that will eventually be more useful in more complex versions of the game.

Two-Word Versions

If the game is to be used to teach two-word utterances, the adult selects a set of photographs such that any one picture is not uniquely identified by means of a single word. For example, four photographs — the baby on the rocking horse, the mommy on the rocking horse, the baby in the airplane, and the mommy in the airplane — might be used. When the children have mastered them, pictures of the mommy in the truck and the baby in the truck might be added.

The game may be used to teach *lie down* and *stand up* in combination with a locative if the set of pictures shows the baby lying down in the playpen, standing up in the playpen, lying down in the cradle, and standing up in the cradle. It may be used to teach the prepositions *in* (or *inside*) and *out* (or *outside*) if the set includes photographs of the baby inside and outside the playpen.

Discussion

One disadvantage of this game is that it is impossible to use photographs of peg dolls to depict actions. Peg dolls simply do not look as if they are walking or running. Similarly, they cannot hold things. The ease of manipulating these toys carries with it the limitation of unposeability. If this disadvantage becomes a serious problem, a game using the same toys in an Identical Arrangement Game (chapter 8) may be useful.

Other Themes

Numerous other themes may be used to create large sets of toys and photographs. For example, a farm may have a barn and a dollhouse together with a farmer, animals, a wagon, a tractor, and other farm paraphernalia. Another theme game shows a city street with stores, traffic lights, cars, and people. The main reason to choose one theme rather than another is motivational; children who are involved in a school unit on zoo animals and who take a field trip to a zoo will enjoy a zoo game. Children may simply prefer farms to zoos. It is helpful, however, to design particular sets of pictures to include animals, as toy animals are sometime easier to manipulate than dolls. For example, bendable rubber animals can sometimes be used to depict "pushing" in a way that dolls cannot. Animals on farms are likely to be inside, outside, and on fences. Similarly, bridges may be included because they are useful in depicting locations: Cars and dolls can be on top of and under bridges in a way that can be photographed clearly.

Restaurant (Level II-A)

This entertaining game helps teach the names of foods and the meaningful use of number terms. It also encourages children to produce long conversational turns; the child who wants a variety of play foods needs to convey a variety of information. An immature child who cannot grasp the idea that the foods are not real and must not be mouthed is not ready for this game.

Materials
The food to be "ordered" in the game is plastic or rubber food, such as hamburgers, carrots, peas, french fries, apples, and fried eggs. Two or more toy pieces of food are needed for each type; for example, two or three hamburgers are needed. The game also requires one photograph of each piece of food. If there are two hamburgers, there must be two photographs of a hamburger. A "serving tray" or plate is needed. A screen is used to separate the players.

How to Play

The speaker in the game is a "customer" and has the set of photographs, which function roughly as a menu. The listener is a "waiter" who fills the speaker's order. The players are separated by a screen. The speaker selects a photograph or a set of photographs and places them in some predetermined spot. The speaker then places an order with the listener for those foods. For instance, the speaker might select two pictures of fried eggs, one of a hamburger, and one of peas. The speaker then tells the listener which foods have been selected and how many of each. The listener fills this order by arranging the requested foods on a tray. The screen is removed, the waiter serves the customer, and the customer checks to make sure that the tray contains the same food shown on the photographs. As in other games, the adult facilitates the play, points out matches or mismatches, and otherwise monitors the playing.

Vocabulary Version (Level I-C)

A simpler version of this game involves only one piece of each kind of food and only one photograph of each piece. The speaker or customer, then, simply names one food to play.

Note on Materials

Plastic fruit and vegetables are common items in preschool classrooms, probably because they are included in several kits and units marketed to preschools. This game, however, is best played with hamburgers, french fries, and other items popular with children as well as with plastic fruit and vegetables. In particular, children from impoverished areas may seldom have the opportunity to eat the kinds of fresh fruit the toys represent. They are likely to be much more familiar with french fries and hamburgers. They are also more likely to have the opportunity to ask for hamburgers in real situations than to ask for pears and bananas. In addition, real meals do not consist of the collections of fruit and unpeeled vegetables the toys represent. In short, while plastic fruit and vegetables can be used in this game, they should not be the only materials.

For the artistically inclined, a marvelous material for making play foods is a colored modeling clay that is shaped and baked in an ordinary oven. This may be used to fashion sets of food such that any one food defies one-word description: a whole pizza, a slice of pizza, cheese pizza, pepperoni pizza, chocolate ice cream, chocolate chip ice cream, chocolate cookies, chocolate chip cookies, and so forth.

The "Boots" Game (Level II-A)

This game is useful to teach agent-modifier-object constructions, as well as negation used to express absence. Its success is partly dependent on a felicitous choice of toys; the "agents" should be appealing figures.

Materials
The following toys are required: bendable rubber figures (about 6 inches long from head to tail) of the Pink Panther, a giraffe, a horse, and a rabbit. Other available characters may, of course, be used. Two rubber boots that fit on the back legs of the animals are also required. Each of the figures is photographed without the boots, wearing one boot, and wearing two boots.

How to Play
The speaker selects one photograph and uses it to direct the listener's choice of animal and its dress (e.g., *The Pink Panther is wearing one boot.*). Note that it is necessary to specify which animal is being used, whether the animal is wearing boots, and, if so, how many boots.

Birthday Presents

This game has a practical virtue as a Picture-Toy Matching Game: It requires no photographs. The birthday content is, of course, extremely appealing. The only limitation on the game's use is that the children must be able to understand that the presents involved are only "pretend" ones; children who try to open them in the hope of finding toys are not ready for this game.

Materials
The materials for the game are "presents" and "pictures" of the presents. The presents are made from boxes of two different sizes; smallish boxes in which tea bags, paper clips, and other such things are packed will do. The absolute size of the boxes is unimportant; the contrast between the big and small boxes, however, must be marked. The boxes are gift wrapped and the wrapping may be designed to elicit multiword utterances — for example, large and small boxes wrapped in red paper and white paper, with and without ribbons. Patterned paper may be used to introduce the need for many kinds of language — red paper with tiny white circles, similar blue paper, red paper with snowflakes, red paper with bells, and so on. Different wrapping paper plus different kinds and textures of ribbon will yield fancy combinations.

The pictures of these presents consist of index cards on which matching paper (and ribbon, if included) is glued. There is one such picture card for each present. The large presents are represented by cards entirely covered with wrapping paper, while the small presents have small squares or rectangles of wrapping paper in the middle of the blank card.

How to Play

The speaker has the cards, and the listener has the presents. The speaker selects one card and uses it to tell the listener what he wants: "For my birthday, I want a big present." The listener gives the speaker the requested present, and the players verify the correspondence between the speaker's card and the listener's selected present. The players then reverse roles.

Clearly, this game has the potential to generate pleasant rituals and fun not intrinsic to the bare playing procedure. Singing *Happy Birthday* between rounds and otherwise encouraging the fantasy-play quality of the game is a good idea.

If the children are able to cope with the demands of the situation, more than two players may participate. For example, two children may both request presents from the same listener, or one child may ask for a different present from each of two listeners. As children become adept players, they may request multiple presents in a turn.

Summary

In Picture-Toy Matching Games, the speaker uses a set of pictures to direct the listener's manipulation of a set of toys. The players receive feedback by comparing the pictures and the toys. Games in this format foster an interchange among players and encourage the use of language to direct others, to request information, and to provide clarification. Theme games are motivating and particularly useful in teaching two-term and multiterm grammatical constructions in a structured context.

Identical Arrangement Games

In Identical Arrangement Games, players use identical sets of toys or pictures. The players are separated from one another by a screen. One player arranges the toys or pictures and describes the arrangement. The other player tries to duplicate the first player's arrangement. The screen is removed, and the players check to see whether the arrangements are identical. This format is, in short, that of classic referential communication tasks or "barrier" games.

Identical Arrangement Games vs. Picture-Toy Matching Games

This format resembles that used in Picture-Toy Matching Games, but it has several advantages and disadvantages when compared with that format. The main advantage of Identical Arrangement Games is flexibility. When photographs are used, the players are limited to the arrangements shown in the photographs. Furthermore, the children do not initiate the arrangements but must follow those an adult photographer has decided on. When toys are used, the child has the chance to make any arrangements he likes. Similarly, the adult may introduce many variations.

On the negative side, the adult loses some control in Identical Arrangement Games. The child is free to make whatever arrangements he likes, so the adult controls only his or her own arrangements. Because of their freedom to arrange the toys, children may find this format difficult. They may have a hard time thinking up arrangements. They may also create arrangements that they then find difficult to describe. If two children play together, a child's description of a complicated arrangement may be hard for the listening child to follow.

Although these games may be somewhat challenging for children, they are also highly entertaining. Furthermore, the situations created in these games are very close to ordinary conversational situations involving children. When children engage in free play, they tell other children what to do with toys. In play, there is no predetermined model of what to do with toys — nothing equivalent to a photograph. Rather, children decide what to do and decide what to tell others to do. The flexibility and freedom of this format, then, resemble the flexibility and freedom of ordinary play, while the game introduces considerably more structure and more demand for language than is found in ordinary play with toys.

Identical Arrangement Games

Players

Children learn to play in one-to-one play with an adult, then two children play together.

Prerequisites

The children must be able to manipulate the toys adequately. They must perceive the match or mismatch between sets of toys. Furthermore, they must be able to think up arrangements of toys and at least try to provide verbal descriptions of those arrangements. Because these games are somewhat challenging, a child must be able to tolerate partial successes, long waits while others arrange toys, and other frustrations. This somewhat challenging format is particularly suitable for children diagnosed as language-delayed without notable cognitive delay or impulsive behavior.

Superheroes and Dinosaurs
(Level II-B and III-B)

This game is effective in eliciting a wide variety of constructions used in different speech acts.

Materials

Each player has a small toy Batman and Incredible Hulk, a toy black dinosaur and green dinosaur, plus a small boat that will, if need be, accommodate all of the other toys. A screen or barrier is needed to separate the players; a manila folder, large box, or folding bulletin board will do.

How to Play

The adult places the screen between the speaker and listener. The speaker arranges the toys, then tells the listener how to arrange his toys similarly (e.g., *The Hulk is riding on the black dinosaur.*). When the listener is ready, the screen is removed, and the arrangements are compared, as in other communication games.

The adult usually begins as the speaker. When a child is first learning to play, the directions may be very simple (e.g., *Batman is riding on the black dinosaur.*). As the child masters the game, complex descriptions involving compound subjects and compound sentences are appropriate (e.g., *Batman and the Hulk are riding in the boat, and the dinosaurs are fighting.*). As the child becomes increasingly competent, the directions may be more and more specific (e.g., *The dinosaurs are fighting. Their heads are together.*).

When the child is the speaker, the adult finds many opportunities to ask for clarification and to check on the adequacy of communication. For instance, the child may refer to a dinosaur, so that the adult must ask, "Which one?". The adult prompts for adequate communication (e.g., *The green dinosaur or the black dinosaur?*). The adult playing the role of listener may also describe his or her arrangement before the screen is removed so that the child has the opportunity to provide corrections (e.g., *Let's see. I have Batman riding on the black dinosaur and the Hulk riding on the green dinosaur. No one is riding in the boat.*).

When two children play together, the adult may, at first, need to provide many restatements of children's descriptions and directions. The adult may also need to request clarification from children. Children often arrange the toys in complex ways that are difficult for them to describe. The adult facilitates communication by providing words for these arrangements; the usefulness of this provision is usually evident when the children immediately

pick up on and use words the adult suggests. The process is evident in the
following excerpts from this game:

> *Brad*: Put dinosaurs biting them.
> *Adult*: Biting each other?
> *Brad*: Yeah.
> (Five minutes later:)
> *Adult*: You only told him about Batman.
> *Brad*: Put Hulk in, too. In boat. And two dinosaurs biting each other.

The adult's provision of the phrase "each other" clearly filled Brad's
communicative need, and he put the phrase to use at the next opportunity.

Discussion

This challenging game elicits many action verbs, used both as directives
(*Make Batman....*; *Put the Hulk....*) and as descriptions (*Batman is
riding....*; *The black dinosaur is biting....*). Complex arrangements of toys
necessitate the use of compound subjects and sentences (e.g., *Batman and the
Hulk....*; *Batman is riding on the black dinosaur, and the Hulk is riding on
the green one.*). Agent-action-object constructions are often necessary.
Various kinds of negation are also elicited, especially when one toy is less
interesting than others and the children want to omit it (e.g., *No one is in the
boat. No boat.*). Possessives are also called for; it is often necessary to say whose
tail is being bitten, and so on.

During the game, it is usually necessary to request clarification and to
provide clarifying feedback and corrections. Interestingly enough, providing
clarification seems to be effective in eliciting the kinds of full sentences that
conventional language therapy tries to elicit by demanding repetitions (e.g.,
This is a....). In playing this game, for instance, Brad and Freddie had lost
touch with each other's topics of conversation:

> *Freddie*: King Kong have big [unintelligible string].
> *Brad*: No. He's not King Kong. That's Hulk. This is Batman. This is a boat.
> That's the dinosaur. That's a dinosaur, too.

Brad is not pointlessly labeling objects when he says "This is." Rather, he is
marking his talk as a particular kind of speech act, and he is using language to
encode information about his relationship with Freddie. Specifically, he
communicates the idea that Freddie is mixed up about which toys are the joint
subject of conversation, and he takes the role vis-à-vis Freddie of the well-
informed person who straightens out the poorly informed person. His speech

encodes the pragmatic presupposition that he knows what's what, whereas Freddie does not. Consequently, Brad has a reason to use "This is a boat" rather than *boat*. *This is a* means, among other things, *I know what this is, but you evidently do not. Consequently, I am informing you about what this is so that you do not continue to disrupt our joint activity.*

Other Versions

Other versions may be simpler or more complicated than that described above. A very simple game is played with a small set of toys: one animal and one toy cage for each player, for instance. With these materials, the speaker may put the animal inside the cage, on top of the cage, or outside the cage. He may have the animal stand up or lie down. The cage may be placed upside down. The animal may be held in the air so that it "flies." Similarly, this format may involve materials that the child uses in everyday life, such as plates, glasses, and silverware. The spoon may be on the plate or next to it. The glass may be on the plate or next to it. This version helps children learn the names of eating implements; it also helps teach locatives.

Multiformat Materials

The Picture-Toy Matching Games described in chapter 7 may be used to prepare children for equivalent games played in the Identical Arrangement format. A Picture-Toy Matching Game may be transformed into an Identical Arrangement Game by adding a duplicate set of the toys and omitting the photographs. In the Picture-Toy Matching Game, the child learns to talk about the toys in a structured context. The photographs provide models of arrangements, and the competent speakers provide models of language to describe those pictures. When the child begins to use the same toys in the Identical Arrangement format, he knows some possible arrangements of toys and some effective ways to talk about these arrangements.

Picture Sequence Games (Level III-A)

Picture Sequence Games help children comprehend and produce utterances used to encode information about the order in which events have occurred.

Materials

Each player has a set of two or three pictures showing the same character or object in a slightly different state or situation. Open-ended sequential pictures are ideal; there must be no fixed order in which the depicted events occur. Each player must have the same set of pictures as the other player or players.

Each player also has a tray or shallow box large enough to hold two of the cards or pictures. (The top of a shoe box is suitable.) This tray is marked with the numerals "1" and "2." On the left-hand side of the tray, "1" is written on the bottom; "1" is also written on a card attached to the tray above the left side. The right-hand side of the tray is similarly marked with "2."

Prerequisites

The point of this game is to help the children encode and decode information about what happened first and what happened later. Consequently, the children must be able to describe and understand descriptions of the pictures alone. Furthermore, the children must be able to master the convention of representing "first" and "second" (or "then") in the left-to-right order marked by the numerals and the places in the tray.

How to Play

The adult must carefully explain the left-to-right, numbered convention of the game. If a picture is placed in the left side of the tray, marked "1," then what that picture shows happened first (e.g., if the duck swimming in the water is under the "1," on the left, then *First, the duck went swimming.*). Whatever is shown in the picture on the right, under the "2," happened later (e.g., *Then the duck got out of the water.*). The adult should use a single pair of pictures to tell little stories explaining the game. For example, the adult must show the child that no particular order of pictures is required. The duck may first swim, then get out, or the duck may stand on the land and then go swimming.

The adult then takes one tray and one pair of pictures and gives the other tray and pair of pictures to the child. A screen separates the players. The adult then "tells a story" while arranging the two pictures accordingly (e.g., *First the duck went swimming. Then, the duck got out of the water.*). The adult encourages the child to arrange his own pictures and to tell the same story. When the child has arranged the pictures, the two trays are compared. The child then has a chance to arrange the pictures and to tell the story that the adult must show in his or her tray.

Vinyl Picture Materials

Identical Arrangement Games may be played with duplicate sets of Colorforms, UniSet play boards, or other similar toys. These consist of a large, flat picture showing a background scene and a collection of vinyl figures that adhere to the large picture. For instance, the background scene may be a schoolyard, while the vinyl figures are children, sand castles, shovels, tricycles, and such. The background may be a farmyard, and the figures may be animals and farm equipment.

These materials require considerable mastery of the conventions of pictorial representation. A background Cookie Monster, for example, appears to be holding a vinyl cookie only if one understands that placing the cookie on the Cookie Monster's hand represents holding. The placement of objects on, in, and next to background landmarks and characters may be unclear to some children. A child's ability to deal with these conventions is readily apparent in play with these materials. Obviously, children who cannot grasp the conventions enough to play should not use these kinds of Identical Arrangement Games.

A problem with some brands of play boards is the provision of dismembered characters that children are supposed to put together on the board. For example, a superhero or cartoon character set may have as vinyl figures the torso, head, and limbs of the characters. The overall effect of these materials is grotesque.

When using play board materials in Identical Arrangement Games, it is important not to provide the children with the full set of vinyl figures. Rather, the adult selects one or two figures for the child. Children who have some experience using a play board enjoy selecting the figures themselves. Linguistically advanced children may be able to play using a rather large number of figures requiring complex descriptions.

There are several advantages to using these play boards. They are considerably less expensive than sets of toys. They are flat and easily carried from place to place. They are also very attractive and provide novelty.

The play boards are used in the same way that toys are used in other Identical Arrangement Games. Players have identical play boards and small sets of vinyl figures. The speaker arranges the figures on a play board and describes the arrangement to the listener, who tries to duplicate it. The players then compare play boards.

Characters and Actions
(Level II-A and III-A)

This game is more highly structured than many other Identical Arrangement Games. Consequently, it is an appropriate game for introducing children to this format. Because the toys used in this game show actions but do not require posing or other manipulation, the game is particularly appropriate for children with difficulties in fine motor skills.

Materials
The game is played with two identical sets of small (2½ inch) rubber toys
showing several different characters performing the same actions. For
example, the toys might show Character A playing tennis, Character B
playing tennis, Character A running, Character B running, Character A
dancing, Character B dancing, Character A kicking a ball, Character B
kicking a ball, and so on. A third character performing some or all of the
actions may be used as well. A screen is used to separate the players. Some
object to mark the choice of character is also useful — a block, a piece of felt, or
some other object.

How to Play
Each player is given one set of toys, and a screen separates the players. Each
player also has a location marker, such as a block. The speaker selects one of
the toys and places it on the block. He then tells the listener which toy he has
selected. The listener tries to pick the same toy; he places the chosen toy on his
block. The screen is removed, and the players check to see that the two toys are
identical.

Introductory Version
This game may be played as a very simple Level I game to teach the names of
the characters, the names for the actions the characters perform, or the names
of the objects they are using. In the very simple version, each player has only
two toys (e.g., Character A running and Character B running). The speaker
then needs to tell the listener only one piece of information (i.e., the name of
the character).

Locative Version
In a complex variation of this basic game, each of the characters may perform
a variety of actions in a variety of places. In addition to the basic materials,
each player has a number of rugs or other objects that show location: a piece of
linoleum, a large red rug, a small red rug, a large black rug, a small black rug,
a square rug, and a round rug. The speaker selects a toy and places it on one of
the possible location markers. He then tells the listener who is doing what
where.
     If the toys are chosen carefully and if many locations are available, this
game may become very demanding. For example, suppose that the game is
played with a boy mouse, a girl mouse, and a cartoon cat figure. Each figure is
shown dancing and sleeping. Each may be placed on a large or small, square
or round, red or white rug. If the speaker selects one of the mice, the listener
must be told six pieces of information: that the character is a mouse, which

mouse, whether it is dancing or sleeping, the size of the rug, the shape of the rug, and the color of the rug. Obviously, such a very complicated version would be played only with children who had considerable experience with simpler versions.

Pepperoni Pizza

A major advantage of Pepperoni Pizza, developed by Zovig Kanarian at the Little People's School in Newton, Massachusetts, is that children can participate in making the materials no matter how poor their fine motor skills. Ms. Kanarian suggests embedding the game in the context of fantasy play: pretending to make pizza. The game illustrates the application of a communication game format to small group work in an academic content area, mathematics. The difficulty of the game may be adjusted by controlling the number of pieces of "pepperoni" available; only a few per player or as many as the "pizzas" will accommodate.

Materials

The materials needed to play the game are circular pieces of heavy paper, colored red (pizzas); many small brown circles (pepperoni); plus screens to separate the players.

Children able to use scissors may cut the large circles out; alternatively, the adult may supply the circles. The children color the circles red; in the context of play, they are putting tomato sauce on the pizzas. Notice that a child who simply scribbles with a red crayon or marker can do a perfectly acceptable job. Adept children may also cut small circles to represent the pepperoni.

How to Play

The children engage in play about making pizza. When the pizzas have been made, they pretend to bake them, and so forth. The object of the game is to have all the pizzas have the same number of pepperonis. Each player takes his pizza and a collection of the pepperonis. Screens separate the players. The first speaker puts one or more pieces of pepperoni on his pizza and tells the others how many pieces he has used. They place the required number on theirs, then everyone examines all the pizzas.

Checking to see whether everyone has the same number involves repeated counting of the pieces of pepperoni; this repeated practice takes place with actual objects, and it has a point in the game. When this game is used with math lessons, the adult must be careful to turn the game over to the children and must make sure that the speaker role is switched at the end of each round of the game. The teacher must not monopolize the speaker role.

Variation
Pizza may, of course, have toppings other than pepperoni, so players may use pretend mushrooms, slices of pepper, and so forth in addition to the pieces of pepperoni. These additional toppings increase the linguistic demand of the game: *three mushrooms, ten pepperonis, and one anchovy.*

Identical Pictures

Ann Hardiman, a language and speech pathologist with the Watertown, Massachusetts public schools, uses the Identical Arrangement format in work with children capable of representational drawing.

Materials
The materials are paper, crayons or magic markers, and a screen.

How to Play
Each player has a piece of paper and an identical set of markers. The screen separates each player's view of the other's paper. The speaker draws a picture on his paper and describes it to the listener, who tries to duplicate the speaker's picture. The screen is removed, and the children compare the drawings.

This may be a group game with one speaker and multiple listeners if the players sit so that they cannot see each other's drawings.

Variations
The use of different sets of materials results in many variations. The speaker may be given a "predrawn" picture that he uses to tell the listener what to draw; in this version, only the listener or listeners do the drawing so a child with poor fine motor skills may function as speaker. Ditto sheets intended to teach listening skills or to give children practice in following directions may also be used. These ditto sheets typically show a scene, with directions for coloring the figures in the scene or for completing the scene (e.g., *Color the bird red.*). The speaker is given a completed ditto and instructs the listeners to duplicate it.

If the speaker's materials are black and white or if colored chalk is available, the listener may duplicate the speaker's picture on a chalkboard rather than on paper. Alternatively, the speaker and listener may be provided with cutouts that can be combined to form pictures: a triangle, rectangles, squares, and other shapes that can be put together to make a house, for example.

Notes on the Screen

In Identical Arrangement Games, a screen of some kind is placed between the players. A player's view of the other player's toys is blocked by the screen so that the arrangements can be duplicated only if the players communicate verbally. The adult may enforce the rule that players not look over or around the screen or may tolerate a fair amount of peeking. Two kinds of peeking occur: The speaker peeks to see whether the listener is complying with instructions, and the listener peeks to see whether he understands the speaker correctly. Allowing children to violate the no-peeking rule is sometimes a good idea.

The child who peeks to see whether the listener is complying gains information that results in corrective feedback to the listener. For example, if the speaker has told the listener to put Batman on the black dinosaur, the speaker may then peek and observe that the listener has used the wrong superhero. In that case, the speaker may say, "Not the Hulk. Batman." The listener, in turn, hears about his or her comprehension error immediately and clearly. Furthermore, with this kind of peeking, the toys provide an immediately perceptible nonlinguistic context that may facilitate the comprehension of the other player's utterances. For instance, *Not the Hulk* can be mapped to the referent Batman. Similarly, the listener who peeks as well as listens may gain information that aids in decoding the speaker's statements. The same information is available simultaneously from looking at the toys and listening to the speaker. This redundancy may help the child decode the speaker's verbal communication.

The best guide about whether to tolerate major violations of the no-peeking rule is the quality of the children's verbalization. If the children continue to provide verbal descriptions and directions, then peeking may supply helpful redundancy and should be tolerated. On the other hand, if the children show the toys and peek at the toys instead of verbalizing, the rule should be enforced. A good index of the need to enforce the rule is children's use of expressions like *This one*, *Put it here*, and *That one*, which do not make meaning explicit. In the former situation, the screen is left up as a reminder to the children to verbalize; in the latter situation, the screen is necessary to point out to the children the necessity of using words.

Summary

In Identical Arrangement Games, the players are separated by a screen. The speaker arranges a set of toys and tells the listener how to arrange a duplicate set identically. In this format, the children initiate the arrangements about which they communicate. The format provides some of the flexibility, freedom, and opportunity for initiation found in naturally-occurring play situations but introduces more structure and demand for language than free play.

9
Action-Directive Games

In these games, one player directs another player to perform various actions. Some of these games are played using photographs of the players; some are played using a screen to separate the players. A challenging game, Cooperative Arrangement, relies on the players' ability to provide feedback without using either photographs or model arrangements.

Picture Positions
(Levels II-A and III-A)

This game helps children learn to direct others and helps to teach prepositions and verbs of motion and position in a particularly active way. The speaker uses photographs of the listener to direct him. If the photograph shows the listener sitting, for example, the speaker tells the listener to sit — then the players use the photograph to verify the adequacy of communication. Because the game involves photographs of the players themselves, the children can be involved in the process of constructing the game materials. The photographs are, of course, interesting and motivating to the children.

Materials

The game requires two sets of photographs. One set shows Player A sitting on a chair, standing next to the chair, standing behind the chair, sitting next to the chair, and lying under the chair. The second set shows Player B in exactly the same positions in relation to the same chair. More players may be included if photographs of those players are taken; one set of photographs is required for each player.

How to Play

If an adult and child are playing, the adult begins by selecting one picture of the child. The child stands near the chair shown in the photographs. The adult directs the child to do whatever he is shown doing in the photograph (e.g., *Here you're sitting in the chair. Sit in the chair.*). The adult rephrases the directions as needed (e.g., *Climb up on the chair. Don't stand in front of the chair, get up on the chair.*). When the child complies or appears to think he has complied, the adult walks up to the child and displays the picture. If all has gone well, the adult points out the match between the child's position and that shown in the picture (*Good. In the picture you're sitting in the chair, and now you're sitting in the chair.*). As in the other communication games, when a mismatch occurs, the mismatch is simply pointed out.

Variations

In a slightly different version, which may be combined with the game described above, the children or children and adult are photographed assuming different positions: touching their toes, standing up, sitting down, lifting their hands up in the air, and so on. If the space available for playing the games is suitable, the children may also be photographed in different places in the room. They then take turns directing one another to the doll corner, to the teacher's desk, to the sink, and so forth.

Discussion

In this format, the children learn to comprehend and produce directions about positions and locations in a way that is very close to natural communicative situations. The child is told to *sit on the chair* and *go to the sink* in much the same way he is told to do these things in everyday life. The learning that occurs in games using this format is active and experiential; the child learns *under* as he actually crawls under something or tells someone else to do so.

This format has one particular advantage over many other communication game formats: Showing the photographs to the other player is ineffective since the players are located too far away from one another for the listener to see the pictures well. Furthermore, efforts to communicate information by pointing and gesturing are not successful. The speaker who holds up a picture, points in the general direction of the listener, and says, "Over there" soon learns that the listener cannot understand what to do. The adult must prevent the speaker from going up to the listener and showing the picture close up, but otherwise the adult need not pay much attention to enforcing the *use words* rule. This format, then, is particularly appropriate for children who chronically try to show pictures and to point. Another particularly effective use of this format is in work with a passive child who never seems to use language to tell other people what to do.

Do What I Do
(Levels II-B and III-B)

Two players are located so that they cannot see but can hear one another. The speaker does something and instructs the listener to do the same thing. The players then check to see whether they have succeeded in duplicating each other's actions or positions.

Materials

The only material required is something to block the children's view of one another. The adult may hold a large piece of cloth between the players. If no suitable screen is available, the players may face in opposite directions.

How to Play

The adult places the children so that they cannot see one another. The adult helps one child to do something: to jump up and down, touch his toes, sit on the floor, or do something else. The adult then helps this child to tell the listening child how to do the same thing. When the listener responds, the adult removes the screen or otherwise lets the children compare actions or positions. The adult may occasionally take a turn playing to model new actions.

Other Versions

This game becomes quite complex if the children do more than one thing at a time (e.g., jumping while putting one's hands on one's head, clapping hands while sitting down) or perform actions in different places (e.g., on a mat or on the floor). Each player may have a chair, and the player directing the action may sit on the chair, in front of the chair, and so forth.

One of the main advantages of this format is its usefulness in helping children comprehend and produce verbs. Static images do a poor job of representing actions like jumping, running, bouncing a ball, and so forth. Children must learn to understand the conventions by which a static image represents action before they can be expected to use these pictures in comprehending and producing language. In contrast, a child actually jumping is immediately communicative.

The Puzzle Game

This game, devised by Jean Berolzheimer at the LABB preschool, Bedford, Massachusetts, illustrates the transformation of a noncommunicative, solitary activity into a communicative, social one.

Materials

The game is played with an insert puzzle in which each piece shows a complete scene or object. The particular puzzle must be one with which the players are familiar.

How to Play

The listener has the pieces of the puzzle, while the speaker has the puzzle frame. Using the empty spaces in the puzzle frame as visual cues, the speaker requests the pieces needed to complete the puzzle. The players then change roles.

One or more players may share the speaker and listener roles, taking turns asking for and supplying pieces. Some children may need considerable prompting from the adult bystander or alternate to learn to formulate the requests for the pieces.

Animal Babies

This game uses the self-correcting feature of materials as a means of providing feedback about communicative effectiveness.

Materials

The game is played with a set of interlocking two-piece puzzles in which one piece shows an adult animal and the other shows the baby of that species. The two pieces interlock only if an adult and its baby are correctly matched.

How to Play

The speaker has the adult animal pieces while the listener has the baby animal pieces. The object of the game is to pair up the parents and children. The speaker selects one piece and asks the listener for the corresponding baby (*I'm a mommy cat, and I want my baby.*). The listener provides the baby, and the players check the communication by fitting the pieces together. If the match is incorrect, the pieces do not interlock. The speaker continues to ask for baby animals until all the puzzles are complete. The players reverse roles. As in all games, children must not remain in any one of these roles.

Who Won the Trophy

Cathleen Cuneo, field coordinator of the project that developed this program, created this game. It is most easily played with only two players, but three or four children may play with adult supervision.

Materials

The game is played with a playing board, tokens that move on the board, a stacked deck of picture cards, and a duplicate deck. The board shows a path leading from a starting point to a finish, which shows a trophy. There are about 14 spaces on which players may land between the start and finish. Each of these spaces shows a character engaging in some sport. This board may be constructed using a 12 by 16 inch piece of cardboard, or an available game board may be adapted. The spaces on which the tokens land are marked by stickers showing sports figures, and a drawing of a trophy or a small plastic trophy is glued onto the finish point. A collection of different brands of sports stickers provides a set of pictures varying in one or more dimensions (e.g., a boy skiing, a girl skiing, a familiar cartoon character skiing, a man playing hockey, a boy playing hockey).

The deck of cards contains as many cards as there are spaces on the board. There are also cards showing a picture of a trophy — one such card for each player. Each card is numbered on the back to correspond to the space on the board where the picture appears. If the first space shows a baseball player, the first card has the baseball player seal on the front and the number "1" on the back, and so forth. The deck is stacked so that the first card drawn is number one, the second number two, and so on. At the bottom of the stack are the trophy cards.

Small dolls representing children make good tokens for this game, such as a boy and a girl. A duplicate set of the cards is also needed; it is not necessary to number this deck. Finally, a small cloth bag or other container for hiding one card is needed.

Setting Up the Board

The adult secretly selects one card from the unnumbered deck and places it in the bag. The bag is placed on the playing board at the finish, next to the trophy. The bag contains the surprise ending of the game: It shows which of the characters depicted on the stickers won. The winner is not one of the child players, but one of the characters shown on the cards and the game board. The numbered deck is placed face down on the playing surface so that the first card drawn is card one. The tokens are placed at the starting point on the board.

How to Play

The speaker draws the top card and, without showing it to the listener, tells the listener where to move the speaker's token (e.g., if the speaker's token is a boy doll and the first space shows a baseball player, *My boy wants to play baseball.*). The listener moves the speaker's token, and the speaker and listener compare the card with the sticker shown on the board. The players reverse roles and do so continuously; the tokens are moved around the board. At the end, the players draw the trophy cards and move the tokens to the finish. The adult and children open the bag to find out which of the characters the players have "watched" in sports competitions has won the trophy. The appearance of the card showing the winner is usually greeted with cries of congratulations for the winner (*Miss Piggy won!*). This "winning" is obviously arbitrary and utterly senseless to adults, but children love the surprise and excitement of the revelation, and the adult must remember that that, in itself, is the real point.

Other Communicative Board Games

Anne Hardiman and Cathleen Cuneo have demonstrated that a minor change in the usual playing procedure transforms some board games into communicative ones. Not all board games, however, are suitable. The most suitable are games in which each player's move is determined by the card he or she draws from a deck. In conventional play, the player moves his or her token to a square on the board matching the drawn card. A suitable game is Milton Bradley's Candyland, in which players draw cards showing colors; if the player draws a card showing a red square, he moves his token to the next red square on the board. Some cards show two squares, and a few show pictures of places in the imaginary Candyland. Any similar game may be used, and new games may be constructed. Games in which moves are determined by dice or spinners are less suitable.

Materials

The required materials are a game board showing a path consisting of colored squares, shapes, or pictures; a token for each player to move along the path; and a deck of small cards showing the same pictures appearing on the board. Note that each picture may appear more than once on the game board and on more than one calling card. For example, in Candyland, there are many squares of each color on the board and many cards for each color.

How to Play

Each player receives a token and places the token at the beginning of the path on the game board. The first player, Player A, is the first speaker. He draws a card and describes it to Player B, the listener, without showing it to Player B. Player B uses the information given by Player A to move his own token on the path. Player A then displays the card, and Player A's card is compared to Player B's position to verify the adequacy of the communication. Player B becomes the speaker, drawing a card and describing it to Player C, who, in turn, moves his own token.

In short, the only difference between the communicative and conventional versions of these board games is the source of information about one's next move. In conventional versions, each player draws his own card and moves his token. In communicative versions, each player is dependent upon someone else for information about what to do.

Conventional board games are always played competitively, and communicative versions are, in general, most appropriate for children who want to play competitive games. These games may, however, be played noncompetitively if the object of the game is to have everyone finish or if one creates some other noncompetitive object.

Up and Down (Level I-A)

This game is used to elicit directives from children who produce no or almost no language. Because the adult lifts the child up and puts the child down repeatedly, only an adult who can easily lift the child should play. Only one adult and one child may play.

How to Play

The adult lifts the child up high, saying "up," then puts the child down, saying "down." After repeating this a few times, the adult puts the child down and asks what to do. If needed, the adult prompts for "up" (*Up? Should I lift you up? Up?*). When the child says anything that can be interpreted as "up," the adult instantly swings the child up. A similar process is used to elicit "down." (The "down" may be more difficult.)

When introducing this game, the adult should move the child up and down frequently regardless of whether the child says anything. Once the child has the idea that the adult will provide this happy tossing up and down, the adult can begin to ask the child for directions.

Sometimes children produce the wrong term. For instance, a child standing on the floor may say "down." The adult should follow the child's directions by putting the child further down on the floor. Similarly, if the child is being held in the air and says "up," the adult lifts the child further up.

This game is a very active, playful one. It is important not to introduce a grim note (e.g., *If you won't talk, I won't do it.*). The idea to get across is this: If you don't tell me what you want, I don't know which action to perform.

Some children are afraid of being lifted high and tossed in the air. If a child shows this fear, try to modify the actions of the game so that the child directs the adult to do something the child likes. Do not insist upon lifting up a child who hates being lifted up. Many children who fear being tossed up high enjoy being lifted up a little bit.

Repeat After Me (Articulation)

This game involves a twist on the conventional speech therapy format of having a child mimic the therapist's articulation of sounds or words. In this game, the adult repeats after the child. The child must be able to grasp the basic idea of the game — that is, to understand that the adult will parrot. The child must also be able to generate something for the adult to repeat. Finally, the child must be able to function in a playing situation that does not involve toys or pictures; a tape recorder can substitute for the usual playthings.

How to Play

The adult explains the basic idea of the game to the child. When the child says something, the adult says the same thing (using clear articulation.). The adult does *not* mimic the child's errors, but translates the child's words into clear speech. If the adult cannot understand the child, the adult cannot perform this translation and hence must ask the child to speak more clearly. This game, particularly suitable for children with serious articulation difficulties, is fun for children who have spent a great deal of time in conventional speech therapy.

A child playing the game may sometimes request that the roles be reversed — that the adult talk and the child repeat. If the child wants to switch roles back and forth this way, the adult may, of course, comply.

Cooperative Arrangement

This activity, devised by Gary Bechtold of the Cambridge-Somerville Mental Health and Mental Retardation Center Preschool, is midway between a game and a generalization activity. The object of the game is to achieve an arrangement of dollhouse furniture and dolls in a dollhouse. The players take turns telling other players where to place the furniture and dolls. There are no photographs or arrangements of toys to be duplicated; the speaker decides where someone else should place a toy, and the speaker evaluates the accuracy of the other player's action. The relatively abstract nature of the game makes it appropriate only for children who can verbalize their intentions about where others should place the toys and who can guide other players in the correct or incorrect following of instructions.

Players

Two, three, or four children may play. The adult may participate as a player or may supervise the children's play.

Prerequisites

This game is suitable for children who have had experience playing structured communication games. The game works smoothly only if children have the cognitive and linguistic skills to think up an arrangement, verbalize their intentions, then provide feedback based on the match between the actual arrangement and their intended arrangement of the dolls. It is not suitable for children with marked cognitive delays. The child who must have a concrete model of how to arrange the toys (e.g., a photograph or an arrangement to be duplicated) in order to describe an arrangemement or to receive feedback about an arrangement is not ready for this game.

Materials

The players sit around an open dollhouse. Any dollhouse accessible to all players is suitable, such as a dollhouse without a roof. The game also requires a set of furniture; a collection of simple, stylized dolls differing in color, such as red dolls, blue dolls, yellow dolls, and green dolls; and two clear plastic bags.

How to Play

One child is declared to be in charge of the materials. This child is the leader of the game for one session and is given one clear plastic bag containing the dollhouse furniture and another bag containing the dolls. The other players take turns asking the leader for selected pieces of furniture. The leader supplies each player with the piece or pieces requested. The other players are not allowed to reach into the bag and grab the pieces, but must tell the leader which pieces of furniture they want. The leader also takes some furniture.

When the furniture has been distributed, the players take turns telling each other which piece of furniture to place in the dollhouse. For example, Child A may tell Child B to put the large chair in the house. Child B may then tell Child C to put in the bathtub.

When the furniture has been placed in the house, the leader proceeds to distribute the dolls. Each player asks the leader for a doll or dolls. The players may take turns requesting one doll each or may ask for specified numbers of dolls in specified colors. The leader also takes some dolls.

The players then take turns telling one another where in the dollhouse to place dolls. Note that it is necessary for players to specify the colors of the dolls (e.g., that a red doll go on the couch, two blue dolls in the bathtub, and so on). The process continues until all of the dolls are in the house. The players then admire the arrangement they have created.

Simplifications and Elaborations

There are several ways to simplify this game. First, the dolls may be limited to one color. Second, the playing may be limited to one piece at a time. Each player may be allowed to request only one piece of furniture or one doll and may be allowed to issue directives about only one piece. In fact, this one-at-a-time version need not be formally decreed but may be modeled by the adult, who may later elaborate the game by modeling multiterm requests. Third, the steps involving the distribution of furniture and dolls may be eliminated. The players may simply be given collections of toys and may then instruct each other where to place the items. Even more simply, the furniture may be arranged in the house before the play begins so that the players arrange only the dolls, not the furniture.

The game becomes complicated if the furniture includes pieces defying one-term descriptions (e.g., two bathtubs or two sofas differing in size or in color). If a double bunk bed is included, the players need to instruct others about whether to put the dolls on the top or the bottom bunk. The adult's modeling of instructions also makes the game challenging. For example, if the players habitually give instructions or requests involving only single items, the adult may break this pattern by requesting two red dolls and one blue doll or by telling someone to put a blue doll in the bathtub and a red doll on the sofa.

This game may involve teaching number terms if players are allowed to request or direct others to place different numbers of dolls. Alternatively, if each player is allowed a fixed number of dolls, the players need to count their dolls to establish their right to request additional ones.

Fast Food, Airport, and Other Content

Different materials may be substituted for the dollhouse and dolls. A game of fast food is played with a toy version of a fast-food restaurant. The toy building is placed on a large piece of felt with pieces glued onto it depicting the parking lot, picnic area, and the lake near the restaurant. The props to be placed in the arrangement include cars, vans, buses, trucks, and boats. Many characters and family pets may visit the restaurant. Similarly, an airport game begins with a toy airport building, and airplanes available in different colors substitute for the dolls in the original version.

Swimming

Susan Morris of the Cambridge-Somerville Mental Health and Mental Retardation Center in Cambridge, Massachusetts designed this game, which is an imaginative way to help children use the names of classmates.

Materials

Close-up photographs of the children in the class are needed. The faces are cut out of the photographs and glued onto paper doll figures made of heavy construction paper or oak tag. A small plastic dishpan or tub represents a swimming pool.

How to Play

The listener has the paper dolls, while the speaker decides who should go swimming. The speaker tells the listener: "Make Joanne go swimming," and the listener complies. The listener then becomes the speaker.

Dress Up

This engaging group game, devised by Jean Berolzheimer at the LABB preschool in Bedford, Massachusetts, helps children use words for clothing in a playful, humorous context.

Materials

The materials are dress-up clothes, such as high-heeled shoes, ballet costumes, a fireman's hat, a cowboy hat, dresses, and jackets. The items may be selected to favor the production of multiword utterances (e.g., a long-sleeved blue shirt and a short-sleeved blue shirt; similar items with and without pockets; furry and silky coats). For a group of children differing in linguistic ability, some items may also be easy to describe using single-word utterances (e.g., the set of clothing might include only one hat). A full-length mirror is also useful.

How to Play

The adult displays the clothing and names or describes each item for the group. The listener stands in front of the group near the clothing. Each of the other children has a turn to tell the listener which piece of clothing to put on. The listener complies. The listener, now arrayed as instructed by the group, may have a chance to admire the result in the mirror. Another child then becomes the listener.

As in all group games, it is important to maintain a lively pace and to avoid playing with a group so large that the children must wait passively for a turn.

Car Wash

Zovig Kanarian at the Little People's School in Newton, Massachusetts devised this game. Children love it.

Materials

All that is required is a chalkboard, chalk, and an eraser.

How to Play

The teacher draws a large outline of a car on the chalkboard. He or she then creates the need to wash the car by drawing or writing on it. If the game is played by advanced children, for example, the teacher may write in letters of the alphabet, numerals, or children's names. The group task is to "wash" the car.

The listener stands next to the chalkboard and is in charge of the eraser. The speakers take turns telling this listener what to wash away. The game continues until the car is completely washed. When the game is first introduced, the teacher is the listener, but the children soon enjoy playing that role.

Snack Time: Beyond the Games

Real-life opportunities for teaching directive uses of language are frequently cited in discussions of incidental, interactive, or directive teaching (Allen, 1980; Hart & Risley, 1975; Rieke, Lynch, & Soltman, 1977). The Action-Directive format provides a paradigm for transforming many everyday classroom activities from noncommunicative to communicative. In particular, the game paradigm is useful in creating communicative situations in which the teacher plays a bystander role rather than a central role. Just as in the games, the teacher may set up the communicative situation and facilitate child-child interaction without acting as a switchboard. The game paradigm also suggests ways to make everyday situations occasions for eliciting multiword rather than single-word utterances.

Kathleen Lockyer illustrates these points during snack time with her class of language-disabled preschoolers in the Watertown, Massachusetts Public Schools. Too often, making snack time communicative merely means making children request food or having them ask a teacher for one of two alternative foods. In Mrs. Lockyer's classroom, snack time is structured to create many different opportunities for various kinds of verbal communication.

Snack is served at one large table. The use of one table instead of a series of small, separate ones places the children in close physical proximity to one another; the physical closeness provides a concrete, structural definition of the situation as a socially and emotionally close one. The resemblance of snack time to a family dinner time is increased further by using place mats. In Mrs. Lockyer's class, the place mats show *Sesame Street* characters. One child is responsible for handing out the place mats, and each person asks that child for the one he or she wants that day. The structure of the situation, then, is that of an Action-Directive Game with one listener and multiple speakers. As in the games, the most salient role is a child's, not a teacher's; the task of handing out place mats rotates among the children. Teachers participate as listeners and facilitators, but they do not co-opt the active, responsible positions.

Deciding which foods to buy and serve is, of course, an adult responsibility. These decisions may maximize the chances for children to use different kinds of language. In Mrs. Lockyer's class, the food available is sometimes selected to form the kinds of sets familiar from the communication games, sets such that any one-word description is ambiguous: chocolate cookies, chocolate chip cookies, and chocolate chocolate chip cookies, for example. Some foods provide alternatives related to preparation: Should the apple be peeled or not? The provision of unusual foods also creates genuine opportunities to ask for information: *Do we like papayas? Do we like them well enough to have them again for snack? Do they remind us of any foods we've had before? Are they good with peanut butter? Who likes them, and who doesn't?* Children also decide how many pieces of food they want. Clearly, the need for elaborate syntax arises when a child may have one, two, or three crackers that may be square or round, with or without peanut butter.

In Mrs. Lockyer's class, children are, whenever possible, responsible for preparing and distributing the food. Adults must, of course, monopolize the use of sharp knives. Children, however, ask one another to make the choices among foods. In practice, it is clear that the movement of the teachers away from the central roles actually places them in extremely active, powerful positions. The teachers, instead of being kept busy distributing food, are free to model conversation, to maneuver linguistically adept children into modeling, and to coach the less able children.

Summary

In Action-Directive Games, the players take turns issuing instructions for action. The speaker tells the listener to perform an action; the listener acts; then the players verify the match between the speaker's intentions and the listener's action. This format encourages children to issue verbal directives for action and is useful in teaching a variety of linguistic content. The Action-Directive format may serve as a paradigm for making everyday classroom situations communicative ones in which there is a real need for multiword utterances and in which children rather than teachers occupy the central roles.

10
Guessing Games

Hiding Games are one form of Guessing Game, primitive kin of familiar games like Twenty Questions. In this chapter, we discuss a structured Guessing Game using a tape recording of sounds. We also discuss some sophisticated Guessing Games played only with words, not with materials. While the Guessing Sounds Game is appropriate for children functioning at low cognitive and linguistic levels, the material-free games are quite demanding. They are, however, highly conversational games that duplicate, in some ways, ordinary conversational interchanges.

Guessing Sounds
(Level I-B)

In this game, the players listen to a tape recording of sounds, guess what makes each sound, then confirm or disconfirm the accuracy of each guess by looking at a picture.

Prerequisites

This game is unsuitable for one-to-one play with a child who cannot recognize pictures or who cannot grasp the basic idea of guessing what makes each sound.

Players

One child, a small group, or even a large group of children may play if provision is made to regulate turn-taking in guessing. This game is especially suitable for groups of children at very different linguistic levels, since children with advanced linguistic abilities enjoy the game and make complicated guesses while the other children make simple, one-word guesses about easily identifiable sounds.

Materials

The required materials are a tape recorder, a recording of familiar sounds, and a set of pictures showing the sources of the sounds. These materials are commercially available. Alternatively, one may make a tape and compile a set of pictures to go with each sound on the tape. Some suggestions for appropriate sounds are: a telephone ringing, a fire engine siren, a car door slamming, a dog barking, a person answering the telephone, a child saying "Hi," the children's morning song, whistling, a car horn honking, and a cat meowing. It is also possible to tape the voices of familiar people: a teacher, classmates, the child himself.

How to Play

The photographs or drawings are arranged in the same order as the sounds on the tape. The first picture is covered up. The adult starts the tape, and everyone listens to the first sound. The children then guess what makes the sound. The game may be structured so that players take turns guessing. Alternatively, different players may make different guesses. When the players have guessed, the adult uncovers the picture. The next sound is then played.

Some sounds are ambiguous or, at best, very difficult to guess. The adult needs to recognize and acknowledge to the children the ambiguity or difficulty of some sounds. The adult may find it impossible to guess what makes some sounds and may say "I don't know." The adult needs to avoid a rigid, overly structured approach to this game. In acknowledging difficulty, the adult has a good opportunity to model the expression of incomprehension or uncertainty, the willingness to guess in spite of uncertainty, and the disagreement with supposed right answers (e.g., *I'm not sure, I don't know, I don't think it sounds like my...*).

This game is reminiscent of tasks used to help children develop auditory discrimination skills. Within the context of a communicative language program, the main advantages of this game are its novelty, its motivational value, and its similarity to real-life communicative contexts. The novelty of using a tape is very appealing to children who have had many therapy sessions involving only visual materials.

Guess and Keep (Level I-B)

This format provides an alternative to Hiding Games when only one set of pictures is available. It provides an interesting variation for children who have used the same Hiding Game materials many times.

Prerequisites

This game requires picture recognition skills but does not require matching skills. For each set of pictures used, *the game presupposes familiarity with that set.*

Players

One adult and one child may play. Alternatively, two or three children may play with adult supervision.

Materials

A set of pictures, exactly the same as for any Hiding Game with Pictures, is required.

How to Play

The adult places the set of pictures face down on the playing surface. One player points to a picture and guesses which picture it is. After he guesses, the picture is turned face up. If the player has guessed correctly, he takes the picture. Another player repeats the process. Pictures guessed incorrectly are replaced face down and remain so until guessed. If the game is played competitively, the winner is the player who has accumulated the most pictures. Otherwise, the point is to remove all of the pictures.

What Did You Do This Weekend?
(Mixed Levels)

Material-free Guessing Games may be used to help children develop the ability to participate in classroom discussions of events that occurred outside the classroom. Circle-time discussions often include children's reports of what happened while they were on vacation or what happened since they were last in school. For example, the children may take turns telling the class what they did at home after school. Children with serious language disabilities experience great difficulty contributing to these discussions. There are, of course, many possible sources of this difficulty. A child may evidently not remember what he did, may be unable to verbalize what he does remember, or may not have a good idea of what might be appropriate conversational contributions. In this game, the adult creates a structured context in which the child succeeds in contributing to these kinds of "What did you do?" discussions. This game is most effectively played in one-to-one work with a single child.

Prerequisites

A child may play this game by contributing only yes-no responses. Because the game is played without materials, the child must be able to attend to the interaction in spite of the absence of appealing toys or pictures. A tape recorder may be used as a substitute for other materials.

How to Play

The adult tries to guess what the child did by suggesting, one at a time, likely activities. For example, if the game is played on a Monday morning, the adult tries to guess what the child did during the weekend. The adult may say, for example, "Let me try to guess what you did at home. You tell me if I'm right, OK? Did you play in the snow?" The adult may interpret even minimal contributions from the child as valid conversational contributions. As the game progresses, the adult may summarize the information he or she has gained. For example, the adult might say, "Let's see. You rode your bike, and you went to church, and you watched TV. What else? Did you have dinner?" The adult may also use the game to model how to relate information about past events. For example, the adult may describe things he or she did that might interest the child: "I went to McDonald's. Do you ever go to McDonald's?" When a child contributes information, the adult may ask for specific details: "You went to McDonald's? Let's see if I can guess what you had to eat there. Did you have a Big Mac? No? Did you have a Happy Meal?"

In this kind of Guessing Game, the adult must adjust the information requested to the abilities of the child. One child may be able to communicate a large amount of detailed information, while another may be able to contribute little. The adult must also be adept at formulating likely guesses. The adult must, for example, have a good set of hypotheses on television shows the child might have watched. Familiarity with the characters on children's television shows is helpful.

If the child is able to play the role of speaker (guesser), the adult and child reverse roles (*Now you guess what I did.*).

Variations

This kind of Guessing Game may be played with many different kinds of content. For example, the adult might try to guess what the child's favorite foods are, what the child got for Christmas, or any number of other things.

It is important to select content that is appropriate to the particular child with whom one is working. One must not try to guess what the child got for Christmas unless one knows with certainty that the child got something. Rather, if one knows that the child's family celebrates Christmas, one might guess what the child did on Christmas, since the child certainly got up in the morning, ate something during the day, played, or watched television.

The Bag Game

Marcia Seletsky, a speech and language pathologist at the EDCO Preschool in Newton, Massachusetts, devised this game, which is particularly enjoyable for groups of children. The general idea of the game is that each player has a bag in which an object is hidden. Each player gives hints to the others about what his or her object is, and the other players try to guess its identity. Some children functioning at very low cognitive levels may be unable to play. The game requires that the players refrain from calling out the names of the objects they are given; some children may be unable to understand or abide by this rule.

Materials

The basic materials for this game are small, brown, paper lunch bags and objects that fit inside the bags. A variety of familiar objects is suitable for hiding in the bags: a mitten, a toothbrush, a tube of toothpaste, a sock, a pair of socks, a fork, a cup, blunt scissors, a belt, a ring of keys, a small book, and such. This game provides a use for irreparably broken cameras and watches.

The objects may be selected for work on particular content, or they may be selected to challenge children's linguistic abilities. For work on articulation, all objects may represent words beginning with a particular sound: a bell, a belt, and a ball. All may belong to one functional category, such as pieces of clothing. In work with older or more advanced children, the objects may be selected for their uncodeability: spools of ribbon and other objects difficult to guess using single words and difficult to hint about without complex talk.

How to Play

The adult and each child have a bag containing an object. The adult tells the children to look in their own bags but not to tell others what they have. The adult demonstrates how to play by giving a hint about his or her object without naming it (e.g., *I'm going to tell you what's in my bag, but I'm not going to tell you the name of it. I'm going to tell you what we do with it. I have something we use to paint with.*). The children then guess what the object is. If they have trouble, the adult provides more clues. When someone guesses correctly, the adult opens the bag and shows the object.

It then becomes a child's turn to provide hints about his or her object. Children almost invariably need to be reminded not to give the name of the object but to tell something about it (*Don't tell us what it is. We want to guess.*). Another task for the teacher is to feed the child potential clues (e.g., *Is it something we wear?*). The game continues until all of the children have had a turn to provide hints about their objects and have the identity of those objects guessed.

Because children may take rather a long time to give hints and to make guesses, it is important to avoid playing this game in a group so large that the children must spend large amounts of time waiting for a chance to do something. The group must be small enough to keep all participants actively involved and interested.

Summary

Guessing Games are a heterogeneous collection of games in which the speaker makes a verbal guess about something. The source of feedback about the accuracy of the guess varies from game to game. Guessing Games range in difficulty from a very easy game in which the speaker guesses the source of a tape-recorded sound to challenging word games played without materials.

11

The Linguistic Content of The Program

The games described in this book may be used to teach a wide variety of semantic and syntactic content. The program may be used to teach specific skills — like the meaningful production of color terms — or may be used to help children develop more general conversational skills. This chapter describes some of the specific semantic and syntactic content that can be taught using the communication games.

Explicit and Implicit Content

The content described in this chapter is content that can be taught explicitly with the communication games. A linguistic element can be taught explicitly with these games only if that element can be used to differentiate between concrete alternatives — that is, if it can be used to make definite reference to one thing rather than to another. For example, color terms can be taught: *Red* is a word that can be used to differentiate between a red object and other objects. In contrast, *This is a...* constructions are not part of the explicit content of this program because one cannot use *This is a...* to achieve definite reference to particular objects. *A cat* and *This is a cat* cannot be used to differentiate between two cats; the two expressions do not communicate information that allows a listener to pick out one particular cat.

Expressions like *This is a...*, modal verbs, exclamations, and many other linguistic items are among the most complicated and pragmatically powerful linguistic elements. While these elements do not serve primarily as encoders of propositional information, they are used to convey many kinds of pragmatic information (Feldman, 1974). Furthermore, while these elements are not taught explicitly in this program, they are taught implicitly in several ways. First, the adult participant in the games models the use of these expressions. Second, the games create situations favoring the production of these markers of pragmatic meaning. For example, the use of the expression *What?* is not taught explicitly. One does not use *What?* to differentiate among referents. When playing the games, however, one repeatedly encounters the need to request clarification. The expression *What?* is probably the simplest lexical means of doing so. While the child is not explicitly taught to ask *What?*, he or she is implicitly taught to do so by being placed in a situation in which that expression is highly functional and in which an alert adult supplies *What?* at times when the child could appropriately use the expression.

Levels of the Program

For heuristic purposes, the content of the program may be divided into three levels of increasing complexity. Level I refers to one-word utterances and includes nouns, modifiers, verbs, quantifiers, and several other classes of words that can be used as one-word utterances. Level II refers to two-word utterances, and it includes simple combinations of elements from Level I, such as noun-verb constructions, noun-noun constructions, and so forth. Level III refers to multiword utterances and modulations, and includes three-term and longer utterances and a variety of expressions used to make meaning highly explicit (e.g., preposition-object constructions).

Level I

The content of Level I consists of words that can be used alone as one-word utterances. Games used to teach Level I content require the use of only one word.

Nouns

The particular nouns taught are dictated mainly by the child's interests and needs. Some categories of nouns are common to all children.

Proper Names

The child is taught to say his or her own name and the names of the therapist, his or her teacher or teachers, and the other children in the class.

Animals

Nearly all young children are interested in animals. Furthermore, children's toys, books, television shows, and other materials feature many kinds of animals. Consequently, children are taught to use names for animals in the games: dog, cat, bunny, and any others that the child seems to want to learn. Which animals to teach the child to talk about depends upon the child's environment. If the child's class is involved in a unit on zoo animals or planning a field trip to a zoo, then the child should be taught to use names for zoo animals. If, on the other hand, the children in the class frequently play with a toy farm, then the child should be taught to talk about farm animals.

In contrast to other approaches to language intervention, this approach helps children use words to express particular meanings, not to produce specific words. Consequently, children are not taught to say *rabbit* rather than *bunny* or *bunny-rabbit*. For the purposes of referring to a rabbit, all of these expressions work. Consequently, what is taught is not any particular word for rabbit, but the meaningful production of any expression that is effective in referring to a rabbit. In many instances, English provides only one word for talking about a particular object; we do not have a multiplicity of words for elephants, tigers, and numerous other animals. Familiar animals like cats, dogs, rabbits, and such, have, however, common diminutive names. Diminutives like *kitty-cat, doggie, bunny-rabbit*, and such are acceptable elements in child language, and there is no functional reason to elicit alternatives. The program does, however, teach comprehension of the adult forms. The adult refers to cats as *cats, kitties,* or *kitty-cats*; however, since the adult can understand the child's production of any of these terms, the adult does not insist that the child produce any particular one.

Food

Children are helped to use words for food mainly because snack and meal times provide children with many conversational openings. The child who can produce words for foods is in a position to say something relevant at meal times. Furthermore, children are almost universally interested in food. Games about food generally include two kinds of content: words for common foods, like milk, juice, and crackers; and words for favorite foods, like hamburgers, pizza, and ice cream.

Familiar Places and Materials

Games can be used to help children talk about the places in their school and the materials used in classroom activities: water fountain, sink, bathroom, potty, Playdough, paper, crayon, magic marker, water, and swing. The particular places and materials to include are determined by the school the child attends and the things the child likes to do. A child who loves to use magic markers should be taught to talk about magic markers, while the child who loves painting should be taught relevant nouns.

Many schools have idiosyncratic names for places in the school, and the children are taught these useful expressions rather than more exact or general names. For example, at one school where this program was developed a large room is used for riding tricycles, playing with balls, and engaging in other gross motor activities. This room also houses a piano. The staff and children at this school call this the "music room," and an outsider experiences some difficulty understanding that the music room is where the children ride tricycles. The children in this school were taught to speak the language of their school — that is, to call the music room "music room."

This example also illustrates the utility of taking one's own photographs for use in the games rather than relying exclusively on commercially available photographs and drawings. No available picture would be an adequate representation of this music room.

Vehicles

Many children express great interest in cars and trucks. The child who can talk about cars and trucks is in a position to make comments while driving places with his family, waiting for a bus, and so on. Furthermore, knowing words for vehicles is helpful to children in their play with other children. Finally, Level II games often involve characters riding in vehicles, pushing vehicles, and so forth. Consequently, children learn to talk about trucks, cars, boats, and, if the child is interested, other vehicles.

People

Besides teaching proper names, the program teaches a few generic terms for people: woman or lady, man, girl, boy, baby. Names of family members may also be taught: mommy, daddy, brother, sister. If the child spontaneously produces any of these terms, the adult player generally uses that term with that child. For instance, if the child refers to *mama*, the adult does not try to elicit *mother*. Adult players, however, do use alternative terms themselves while playing the games, thus encouraging the children to comprehend a variety of terms even though they produce only one.

Seasonal Terms
Holidays generally interest children and provide them with many opportunities to comment on holiday decorations, television shows, advertisements, and such. Children enjoy learning a few key words associated with major holidays. For example, Halloween games show witches, pumpkins, masks, candy, and ghosts. Some schools do not celebrate Christmas, and at these schools it is best to avoid games about Christmas. Seasonal games may be about events other than religious holidays. For example, a winter game may help children talk about snow, snowmen, mittens, and other objects associated with winter.

Classroom Activity Terms
The objects used in classroom circle and meeting times may be used in communication games as well. For example, one classroom where these games were developed has a set of paper cutouts used in the daily monitoring of the weather: a snowman, a dark cloud, an umbrella, and such. These are used in a Hiding Game (chapter 5). The inclusion of content relevant to the child's experience at school helps the child to prepare to talk at the formal class meeting times; the child has a chance to practice talking about snow, days of the week, farm animals, foods, or whatever else the class is currently talking about at meeting times.

Disussion
The general categories discussed above are by no means an exhaustive list of the kinds of content that may be included. In general, two criteria are used to decide which nouns to present to a child. First, children should be helped to talk about things that are of particular interest to them. The most effective way to help children talk is to help them say what they would like to say. The child who loves food is helped to talk about food. The child who loves trucks is helped to talk about trucks. Second, children's opportunities to use language in their everyday lives should be considered. In some schools, teachers place a high value on a child's ability to name body parts, to name zoo animals, or to talk about some other particular content. When this is the case, the children should be taught to use words that will generate a strong positive response from these adults.

Modifiers

In deciding which modifiers to teach, one sometimes encounters a conflict between a child's interests and the values of adults. Children are interested in affect-laden, perceptually salient, expressive qualities, while adults sometimes want children to learn words for numbers and colors. Children are interested in the bigness, tininess, and "yuckiness" of things, while adults sometimes want children to count.

Big and Little

Children are often impressed by gross differences in size. In teaching children to use words for size, it is important to use objects that differ greatly in size — the big object must be very big and the little object must be tiny. To young children, *big* and *little* are not references to subtle distinctions. These terms may be taught in relation to objects that interest children. For example, big dogs and little dogs, big pumpkins and little pumpkins, and big trucks and little trucks are more motivating than big and little circles.

Other Adjectives

Other adjectives that may be taught include *empty* and *full* (glasses of juice; shelves), *pretty* and *ugly* (witches), and *real* and *pretend* (play refrigerators, stoves). In particular, talking about whether things are empty or full provides the child with the chance to use negation: *Empty* means, for children, "all gone." *Chocolate* and *vanilla* are also good choices.

Modifiers may be taught if one can devise a way to show the qualities these adjectives are used to describe. For example, the terms *broken* and *fixed* can be taught by using a small plastic boat made from two pieces of plastic. The boat is taken apart, and several of the slots that hold the boat together are removed with a razor blade. The boat can be "broken" easily by pulling the pieces apart and "fixed" by putting the pieces together. The boat can then be photographed in its broken and fixed states and the toy and pictures used in a Toy-Picture Matching Game (chapter 7).

Colors

As noted above, adults sometimes place a high value on a child's knowledge of colors. Within the context of the communication games, color terms are important because color is an easy way to differentiate among toys — it is convenient to be able to construct games contrasting red and blue boats, brown and white horses, and green and red cars. In teaching color terms, the most frequently encountered problem is one of comprehension. Children often use a couple of color terms (e.g., *red* and *blue*) to describe all colors and respond to color terms in an apparently random fashion. When beginning to teach color terms in the games, then, one uses only two markedly different colors (e.g., red and white or red and blue, but not red and orange, red and yellow, or blue and green). Suppose, for instance, that a child uses *red* to refer to all colors. He then plays a game with only red and white. The game creates a need for the child to refer to something other than red, and the adult player immediately provides the term *white* as a way to do this. The child receives clear and immediate feedback to the effect that *red* works only to refer to the red object, and that another word is needed. Once the child understands and produces these two color terms, a third is introduced. Again, this color term should refer to a color that differs notably from the first two.

Although curricula seldom seem to include the terms *gold* and *silver*, shiny objects are often appealing to children, and these are appropriate words to teach. Furthermore, silver and gold contrast sharply with the colors usually taught; hence, teaching these terms facilitates teaching the more commonplace color terms. *Black* and *white* are useful both in providing contrast and in providing terms that have many uses; toy animals, for instance, often come in both black and white. The child who learns these terms can immediately begin to use them to differentiate between interesting objects.

In teaching color terms, the emphasis is on the comprehension and meaningful production of a limited number of color terms rather than on the production of a large number of terms. The child needs to be able to understand and produce color terms to talk about toys, clothing, and other familiar objects; the ability to perform well in a testlike situation is less important. Consequently, color terms are generally taught as the need arises rather than in programmatic fashion. However, the games may be used in a formal program of teaching the meaningful use of large numbers of color terms.

Quantification

As is the case with color terms, the games teach the comprehension as well as the production of number terms. The games stress the meaningful use of terms for small numbers (one through five) and of quantifiers like *lots of*, rather than the empty production of terms for large numbers or rote recitations.

One vs. "Lots Of"

While children are seldom struck by the contrast between one and, say, three objects, they are often interested in the contrast between one object and a great many objects. Consequently, game materials may illustrate one object and "lots of" the same object: one boot and lots of boots, for instance, are easy to depict.

Numbers

Numbers, like colors, are taught gradually. One game may show one cat and two cats. Another game may show one cat, two cats, and three cats. Another may show one, two, three, and four dogs. Games like these are considerably more interesting to children than games involving geometric shapes or boring objects. Packages of stickers are handy for the construction of number Lotto, Bingo, and Hiding Games. The child who likes dinosaurs can learn to count meaningfully by counting dinosaurs. Children can count hockey players, football players, birds, witches, and anything else depicted on stickers. Similarly, familiar objects can be photographed in different quantities: shoes, boots, crackers, blocks, toy trucks, or anything else available in quantity.

Verbs

Verbs are difficult to teach, partly because actions are difficult to represent in static images. Considerable ingenuity is sometimes required to find toys and pictures that illustrate actions clearly. The easiest verbs to teach in the communication games are verbs used to describe actions that toys can show clearly. Dolls can be made to sit, stand, and lie down or fall down. Toy animals can ride in, drive, and push cars.

Photographs of people are sometimes useful to show actions. One set of photographs used in Hiding and Lotto Games (chapters 5 and 6), for instance, shows a child patting a cat and hugging or holding the cat. Children can be photographed reading or looking at books, looking at toys, holding toys, and so forth.

At Level I, some verbs may be introduced as parts of unanalyzed routines. The children can be encouraged to produce expressions that include verbs, although the games do not absolutely require the production of these verbs. For example, if a picture shows someone eating crackers, the word *crackers* may be all that is needed to identify the picture, but the adult player may model the use of *eating crackers*. Similarly, the phrases *drinking milk, putting on coats,* and *riding bikes* are often used in games in which children could adequately use the nouns in these phrases alone.

Locatives

The simplest way to teach a child to begin to talk about spatial location is to use the Up and Down Game described in chapter 10. That game, in which the child is lifted up and down on his or her command, may be supplemented by games in which *up* and *down* are used as descriptions rather than as requests for action. For example, a child may be photographed holding a toy up and down, and these pictures may be used in a Hiding Game (chapter 5).

In games designed to elicit one-word utterances, prepositions may be taught if one object is placed (or photographed) in different spatial relationships to another object. For example, a toy cat may be shown on, under, beside, and in front of a toy chair or some other object. In teaching prepositions, it is important to remember that in communication games one elicits adequate communication rather than the production of specific, predetermined, forms. One cannot use these games to teach a child to say *beneath* rather than *under*, *beside* rather than *next to*, and so on. If a particular word works in a game, then one does not arbitrarily insist that the child use some other word instead. When possible, one creates a game that necessitates the use of both words, When words are synonymous, however, that cannot be done. One can, however, provide the child with redundant statements that help him or her comprehend alternative terms. For example, one talks about a toy *on the barn* and *on top of the barn* or *next to the cow* and *beside the cow* and otherwise provides the child with information that is helpful in decoding the less familiar terms.

Negation

Bloom (1970) and Brown (1973) describe three kinds of negation: nonexistence, rejection, and denial. That is, children use negation to express nonexistence, absence, or disappearance of someone or something; to express rejection of actions or objects; and to deny propositions. If a child has just finished eating all of the Cheerios on his plate, he may express their nonexistence by saying: *No Cheerios*, *No more Cheerios*, *Cheerios all gone*, or *All gone Cheerios*. If his mother offers him Cheerios, he may reject the offer by saying *No Cheerios*. If his mother puts Rice Krispies on his plate, he may deny their being Cheerios by saying *No Cheerios*.

The use of *no* that may be explicitly taught at Level I is rejection. Specifically, the adult may ask the child yes-no questions in the form "Do you want the _____ one?" The child who answers *Yeah* accepts, and the child who answers *No* rejects this offer. This kind of adult question is a particularly important one in work with language-disabled children for two reasons. First, some language-disabled children produce both *yes* and *no* but seem to use these words as diffuse markers of response rather than as positive and negative responses. The child who says *no* does not necessarily mean "no." Second, some children seem to discover that saying *Yeah* and smiling is an action that yields happy consequences. They cheerfully say *Yeah* in response to most questions without regard for the propositional content of the questions.

Level II

Level II games are designed to elicit two-word utterances. Some of the specific constructions that games may be designed to elicit are described below.

Agent-Object: Noun-Noun

Combinations of two nouns in agent-object constructions are elicited in games in which the speaker must tell the listener which agent and which object are involved in order to differentiate among various possibilities. For example, a set of pictures may show a cat eating crackers, a cat eating ice cream, a dog eating crackers, and a dog eating ice cream. To pick out only one of these pictures it is necessary to specify both the agent and the objective — that is, the cat or the dog and the crackers or the ice cream. In a game designed to elicit agent-object constructions, it is not necessary to specify an action. In the example, it is not necessary to say that an animal is eating.

Agent-Locative

Agent-locative constructions are used to tell the listener which agent is in which place. For example, a set of materials designed to elicit agent-locative constructions might consist of pictures of Child A on a chair, Child A on the floor, Child B on a chair, and Child B on the floor.

Entity-Locative

Entity-locative constructions are used to say which object is in which place. For example, materials for an entity-locative game might be pictures showing a cup on a plate, a cup on the floor, a glass on a plate, and a glass on the floor.

Possessor-Possession

Possessor-possession constructions are used to tell a listener who owns what. A set of pictures designed to elicit these constructions might show Child A's feet, Child A's jacket, Child B's feet, and Child B's jacket.

Agent-Action

These constructions are noun-verb combinations used to specify who is acting and what the action is. For example, a Picture-Toy Matching Game (chapter

7) might use pictures of a toy cat driving a toy truck, the cat pushing the truck, a toy horse driving the truck, and the horse pushing the truck. In this example, the listener needs to know which animal is involved and what the animal is doing if he or she is to pick out the referent.

Action-Object: Verb-Noun

These constructions are verb-noun combinations used to specify an action and the object acted on. A game designed to elicit these constructions might use a set of toys and corresponding pictures showing a superhero driving a car, pushing the car, driving a truck, and pushing the truck. In this example, the listener needs to know what the superhero is doing (driving or pushing) and what vehicle he is acting on (a car or a truck) to match the toys and the picture.

Attribute-Entity

These modifier-noun constructions encode information about some quality and the person or thing that has the quality. *Pretty girl, two cats*, and *yellow circle* are attribute-entity constructions. A game designed to elicit these constructions might be a Lotto Game (chapter 6) using duplicate sets of the following pictures: one cat, two cats, one dog, and two dogs. Another, duller set might show a red circle, a red square, a white circle, and a white square. In the former example, the listener needs to know how many animals and which kind of animal to pick out a particular referent. In the latter example, the listener needs to know both color and shape to be able to pick out the referent.

Negation

Constructions of the form "Negative x" that are used to express nonexistence may be taught. For example, a child may play a hiding game (chapter 5) using two pictures: one showing a girl wearing glasses, the other showing the same girl without the glasses. To differentiate between the two pictures, it is necessary to say *glasses* or *no glasses,* or otherwise to express the presence or absence of the glasses. Other materials may show a child with and without a hat, with and without mittens, and so forth. The design of these materials is tricky, since the pictures used must be identical except for the presence or absence of the object of interest; otherwise, the negation is not necessary. For example, a picture of a boy standing near a water fountain and another picture of the boy drinking from the water fountain will probably not elicit negation. Children are apt to describe these pictures as, say, *standing* and *drinking* rather than as *drinking* and *not drinking.*

Level III

The content of Level III consists of multiword utterances and certain devices for the modulation of meaning.

Multiword Utterances

The constructions described under Level II may be combined to yield three-term and longer constructions. For example, agent-action constructions and agent-object constructions may be combined as agent-action-object constructions. A set of materials to be used in eliciting such constructions might be a toy cat, horse, truck, and car. Photographs would show each animal pushing each vehicle and driving each vehicle. To pick out only one of these pictures, the listener needs to know which animal is doing what to which vehicle. If each toy animal were available in two different colors, modifier-agent-action-object constructions would be needed (e.g., *The brown horse is pushing the truck. The white horse is pushing the truck. The white cat is driving the wagon.*).

Prepositions

The easiest kind of modulation to teach in the communication games is the use of prepositions. The first prepositions young children produce are usually *in* and *on* (Brown, 1973). Language-disabled children often produce these prepositions as diffuse markers of the fact that location is being talked about. *In* or *on* means, roughly, "somewhere in the general vicinity of," and these words are used in place of prepositions like *under, on top of, beside, next to,* and such. The accurate production and comprehension of these prepositions is easy to teach because the spatial relationships these words encode can be shown clearly in arrangements of toys and people and in photographs. Furthermore, such prepositions are the only means English provides for expressing these relationships. It is difficult to say that something is on top of something else without using a preposition.

Contrastive Word Order

Communication games played with toys are a particularly effective way to teach children about contrastive word order — that is, to help children understand the difference between "The dog is biting the cat." and "The cat is biting the dog." Contrastive word order is also evident in the difference between "The cat is on the chair." and "The chair is on the cat."

This kind of contrast is more easily taught using toys than actual objects in real-life situations. Toys may appropriately be placed in improbable positions and made to engage in improbable activities. In actuality, for instance, the cat is unlikely to bite the dog but, in play, cats bite dogs, dinosaurs bite one another's tails, and horses are underneath fire engines.

Discussion

In this book, we repeatedly mention the necessity of communicating certain pieces of information. For example, if a listener is to arrange a set of toys so that a black dinosaur is biting a green dinosaur's tail, the listener needs to know which dinosaur is acting and which is acted on, what the actor is doing, what part of the bitten dinosaur is involved, and so forth. To communicate these simple pieces of information, no one sentence is "necessary." "The black dinosaur is biting the green dinosaur's tail" is a highly efficient way to convey the needed information. It is not, however, the only way to convey this information. Consider a few examples:

1. "Black bite green tail."
2. "Dinosaur bite green tail."
3. "Black bite. Bite green. Green tail."
4. "Black one bite green one. Green tail."

These examples show alternatives to the fully formed sentence. Within the context of a communication game, each sentence might be communicatively adequate. For example, (1) would work if the only choice of toys consisted of two dinosaurs. If a black shark and green shark were also available, then (1) would be ambiguous. If three dinosaurs differing in color were available, then (2) would be ambiguous; the red dinosaur might be doing the biting. Examples (3) and (4) could, of course, be interpreted as ambiguous: The apparent connections among the utterances might be ignored. For example, the listener might not assume that the green tail had something to do with the biting. As in (2), both would be ambiguous if sharks as well as dinosaurs were possible referents.

When children begin to play complicated Level III communication games, they produce the kinds of utterances given in the examples above. As Bloom (1973) shows, children learning to talk begin uttering strings of short utterances; the necessity of conveying certain pieces of information does not immediately result in the encoding of all those pieces of information in single, grammatically elaborate sentences.

In conventional language training, the method used to elicit the more elaborate sentences (e.g., *The black dinosaur is biting the green dinosaur's tail.*) is to request repetitions of the model (e.g., *Say, "The black dinosaur...."*). If this fails, and it usually does, then the adult ordinarily breaks down the model sentence into units and asks the child to repeat each unit (e.g., *Say "The black dinosaur," Say "is biting,"* and so forth). The adult then asks the child to put these strings together to give the full sentence. Obviously, this repetition has nothing to do with conveying information; the child is not even asked to direct his attention to the propositional information encoded in the model sentence.

In the communicative approach, the method used to elicit more elaborate utterances is to elicit the meaningful use of the strings that can be combined to form those utterances. For example, if a child characteristically produces utterances like (1) above ("Black bite green tail "), the adult creates a need to encode additional information. The adult, for example, might introduce a second black animal so that *black* alone would be ambiguous. The adult does not request that the child repeat the model sentence, but helps the child to discover the usefulness of fully formed sentences.

Program Planning

These levels refer to games and their content, not to children. One child may work concurrently on games at different levels. For example, a chronically silent child capable of comprehending and producing multiword utterances may seldom say anything at all. Level I games might be used to help this child produce speech in a minimally challenging situation. Level II games might be used to increase the frequency with which the child produces two-word combinations. Finally, Level III games might be used to help the child work on some specific skills, such as using words to encode exact information about spatial location. Some children may work at one level as listeners and at another level as speakers. For example, a child with expressive aphasia might function only as a listener in Level III games but as a speaker in Level I games.

12
Designing and Constructing Games

This chapter is intended for the teacher, speech therapist, or parent who wants to make sets of materials for communication games. The first section contains material about designing games, and the second section contains practical hints on selecting materials.

The Design of Materials for Level I, II, and III Games

The following example illustrates the design of games to teach one-term (Level I), two-term (Level II), and three-term (Level III) constructions. The example is for illustrative purposes; its content is rather dull for preschoolers. The format is Lotto (chapter 6), and the content is (1) two different color terms (*red* and *blue*), (2) two size terms (*big* and *little* or *small*), and (3) two shape terms (*circle* and *star*). Level I games teach the comprehension and production of these terms as one-word utterances (e.g., *star* or *big*); Level II games, as two-word combinations (e.g., *red circle* or *big star*); and Level III games, as three-word combinations (e.g., *big red circle* or *little blue star*).

Level I

There are 12 possible Level I Lotto Games. The materials for each consist of one master card showing two pictures, together with two smaller calling cards, each of which shows one of the pictures on the master card. The shape cards are as follows, with only the master cards shown:

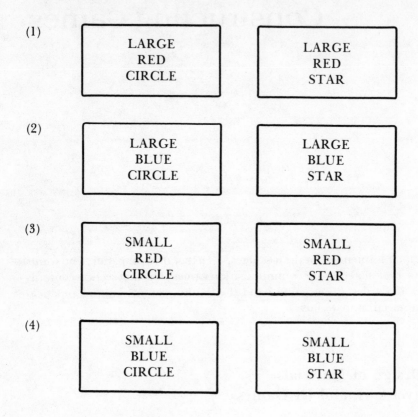

(1)

LARGE
RED
CIRCLE

LARGE
RED
STAR

(2)

LARGE
BLUE
CIRCLE

LARGE
BLUE
STAR

(3)

SMALL
RED
CIRCLE

SMALL
RED
STAR

(4)

SMALL
BLUE
CIRCLE

SMALL
BLUE
STAR

The color cards are as follows:

(5)

SMALL
RED
CIRCLE

SMALL
BLUE
CIRCLE

(6)

LARGE RED CIRCLE	LARGE BLUE CIRCLE

(7)

SMALL RED STAR	SMALL BLUE STAR

(8)

LARGE RED STAR	LARGE BLUE STAR

The size cards are as follows:

(9)

SMALL RED CIRCLE	LARGE RED CIRCLE

(10)

SMALL BLUE CIRCLE	LARGE BLUE CIRCLE

(11)

SMALL BLUE STAR	LARGE RED STAR

(12)

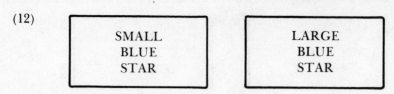

The point is that only one word is necessary to refer unambiguously to one of the pictures on a master card. For example, for Set 1, *circle* refers to the circle. A color or size term does not work. For Set 1, *red* could mean either the star or the circle, as could *big*.

Level II

There are six possible Level II games. The following require that both shape and size be specified; color is held constant.

(1)

(2)

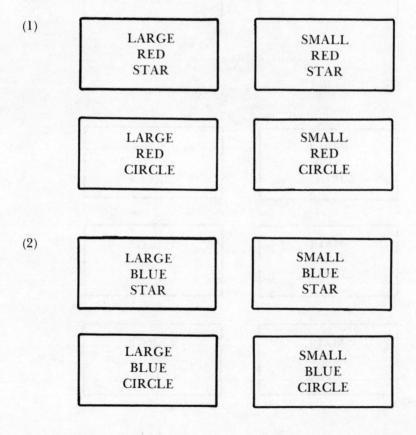

The following require that shape and color be specified; size is held constant.

(3)

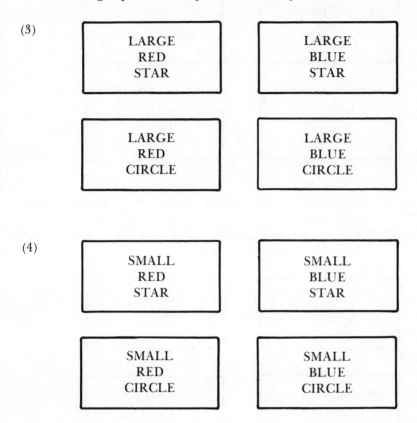

(4)

The following require that size and color be specified; shape is held constant.

(5)

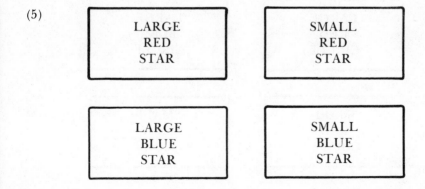

(6)

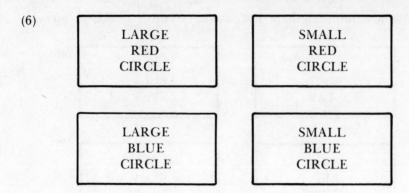

Level III

The Level III game demands the specification of color, size, and shape:

<table>
<tr><td>LARGE
RED
STAR</td><td>LARGE
BLUE
STAR</td></tr>
<tr><td>SMALL
RED
STAR</td><td>SMALL
BLUE
STAR</td></tr>
<tr><td>LARGE
RED
CIRCLE</td><td>LARGE
BLUE
CIRCLE</td></tr>
<tr><td>SMALL
RED
CIRCLE</td><td>SMALL
BLUE
CIRCLE</td></tr>
</table>

Notes about Card Sets

1. Level I Sets 1, 2, 3, and 4 could be reduced to two sets if color were omitted. That is, one master card could show a large circle and a large star, while the other could show a small circle and a small star.
2. The same small calling cards can be used for all the sets: The Level III cards show all possible combinations of shape, size, and color, and can be used for all of the other games.
3. This is a very simple example. It would be possible to use more than two colors and more than two shapes, generating a large Level III game and many more Level I and II games.
4. This example shows what is called in the text a "perfect" or "complete" game. As discussed in the text, such perfection is unnecessary as well as impossible or unlikely when the pictures are of people and animals doing various things. For instance, if one uses a big bird, little bird, a big boy, and a little boy, the birds could fly in some pictures, but the boy could not. The impossibility or improbability of certain situations helps reduce the eventual size of the games. Actual games, then, may vary in a number of different dimensions, but they are likely to show only some possible combinations.
5. The calling cards from this set can be used to play the Hiding Games described in chapter 5.

Planning and Construction

The previous example illustrates the point that Level I games require only one-term utterances; Level II games, two-term utterances; and Level III games, three-term or multiterm utterances. This basic point applies to content that is more lively than the size and color of geometric shapes.

The easiest way to begin designing a series of Level I, II, and III games is to decide on content of interest. For instance, zoo animals are appealing to many young children, so a game might be about zoo animals. The animals in a zoo can perform various actions and hence offer the opportunity to teach verbs. An animal may be large or small, so a game could teach size terms. A toy animal may be placed in various locations, so a game could teach locatives. Furthermore, different numbers of small toy zoo animals could occupy the same locations, so a game could teach quantifiers.

Small toy animals can be hidden in Hiding Games with Objects. Photographs of the zoo animal toys could be used in Hiding Games with

Pictures. Duplicate sets of the photographs could be used to construct Lotto or
Bingo Games. Photographs or drawings of zoo animals could be used for
related Hiding and Lotto Games as well. If two sets of the toys were available,
the sets could be used for Identical Arrangement Games. The toys could be
photographed and used in Picture-Toy Matching Games. In short, the idea
has possibilities for teaching a variety of linguistic content in a variety of
formats.

The next step is to plan specific arrangements of toys to be photographed.
What sets of photographs of zoo animals could be used for Level I, II, and III
games? The easiest way to accomplish this practical planning is to plan some
Level II sets, then to break down those sets for Level I games and to elaborate
them for Level III sets. An obvious Level II set would include these pictures:

- the lion walking
- the lion lying down
- the elephant walking
- the elephant lying down

To specify only one of these four pictures, it is necessary to say which animal is
involved and to say what the animal is doing.

This set breaks down into the following Level I sets, in which any one
picture can be identified using only one term:

- the lion walking
  the lion lying down
- the elephant walking
  the elephant lying down
- the lion walking
  the elephant walking
- the lion lying down
  the elephant lying down

The basic Level II set can also be elaborated to make a Level III set:

- the lion walking in the cage
- the lion walking in front of the cage
- the lion lying down in the cage
- the lion lying down in front of the cage
- the elephant walking in the cage
- the elephant walking in front of the cage
- the elephant lying down in the cage
- the elephant lying down in front of the cage

Many other possibilities suggest themselves. One, two, or three lions could be in a cage for a Level I game. In a Level II game, different numbers of lions could perform two different actions. In a Level III game, different numbers of lions could perform different actions using different objects (e.g., one or two lions driving or pushing a car or truck).

At this point in designing a game, a number of props for the zoo emerge: cages, vehicles, and multiple sets of animals. The next step, then, is to acquire the props. In selecting the toys, one bears in mind the plans for the game. For example, several lions should fit in the cars or trucks, and the cages should have flat tops so that the animals can be placed on top of them without falling off. The search for appropriate toys may suggest new possibilities for the game. For instance, if toy cars differing only in color are available, the game might teach color terms. For Level I, a lion could drive a red car or a black car. For Level II, an elephant or a lion could drive a red car or a black car. For Level III, an elephant or a lion could drive or push a red car or a black car.

The next step is to arrange and photograph the toys as planned. One's efforts to arrange the toys may disclose unforeseen problems. If the animals are difficult to arrange as planned, these arrangements will be impossible for the children, so new plans must be made. The photographs, as discussed elsewhere, must be clear.

Finally, the game should be pilot tested and revised. Pilot testing not only shows unforeseen problems but also suggests elaborations that can be incorporated into the game. For example, children using toys in an Identical Arrangement format sometimes invent new actions and arrangements that can be photographed for use in Picture-Toy Matching Games.

A Detailed Example

The following example illustrates the use of a single large set of materials for playing games in a variety of different formats. The choice of content (superheroes and dinosaurs) is arbitrary. The same games could be played using other appealing content. The point of this example is that a set of materials can be used for different game formats played at different levels.

Materials

The materials for this game are:

- 2 black dinosaurs
- 2 red dinosaurs

- 2 Superman toys
- 2 Incredible Hulk toys
- 2 red boats
- 2 black boats
- toy food (shredded paper will do)
- 1 screen to separate the players

The guidelines followed to select the materials were:

- Superman and the Hulk must be able to ride on the dinosaurs.
- The boats must be able to hold both superheroes simultaneously.
- The boats must be large enough so that a superhero can "liedown" in a boat. Superheroes should be able to "stand" in the boats without falling over too easily.
- Superheroes should be poseable (i.e., able to sit, "push," ride dinosaurs).

Photographs for Superheroes and Dinosaurs Series

The numbers of the photographs listed below are referred to in the lists of games that follow. These particular arrangements of toys and photographs are samples of those that could be used.

1. Superman riding on the red dinosaur
2. Superman riding (sitting) in the red boat
3. The Hulk riding on the red dinosaur
4. The Hulk riding (sitting) in the red boat
5. Superman riding on the black dinosaur
6. Superman riding (sitting) in the black boat
7. The Hulk riding on the black dinosaur
8. The Hulk riding (sitting) in the black boat
9. Superman falling off the red dinosaur
10. Superman falling off the red boat
11. Superman pushing the red boat
12. The Hulk falling off the red dinosaur
13. The Hulk falling off the red boat
14. The Hulk pushing the red boat
15. Superman standing in the red boat
16. Superman standing in the black boat
17. The Hulk standing in the red boat
18. The Hulk standing in the black boat
19. Superman lying down in the red boat

20. Superman lying down in the black boat
21. The Hulk lying down in the red boat
22. The Hulk lying down in the black boat
23. The red dinosaur walking
24. The red dinosaur eating the food
25. The red dinosaur riding in the red boat
26. The red dinosaur riding in the black boat
27. The black dinosaur walking
28. The black dinosaur eating the food
29. The black dinosaur riding in the red boat
30. The black dinosaur riding in the black boat
31. The black dinosaur biting the red dinosaur's tail
32. The red dinosaur biting the black dinosaur's tail
33. The black dinosaur biting the red dinosaur's head
34. The red dinosaur biting the black dinosaur's head
35. The dinosaurs fighting with each other
36. The Hulk and Superman fighting with each other
37. Superman fighting with the red dinosaur
38. Superman fighting with the black dinosaur
39. The Hulk fighting with the red dinosaur
40. The Hulk fighting with the black dinosaur
41. The red boat
42. The black boat
43. The red dinosaur
44. The black dinosaur

Hiding Game with Pictures
(Chapter 5)

A small piece of the dinosaurs' "food" is hidden under one of the pictures. The speaker guesses where the listener has hidden the food.

Level I-B: Games To Teach One-Word Utterances

1. Pictures 1 and 3, 2 and 4, 5 and 7, *or* 6 and 8 call for the use of proper nouns as agents.
2. Pictures 1 and 2 *or* 3 and 4 call for the use of nouns as objects or as locatives.
3. Pictures 1 and 5, 3 and 7, 2 and 6, 4 and 8, *or* 25 and 26 call for the use of color terms.

4. Pictures 2, 15, and 19; 6, 16, and 20; 4, 17, and 21; or 8, 18, and 22 call for the use of the verbs *sit, stand,* and *lie down* or equivalent expressions.
5. Pictures 9 and 10 *or* 12 and 13 call for the use of nouns as objects.
6. Pictures 10 and 11 *or* 13 and 14 call for the use of the verbs *push* and *fall off* or equivalent expressions.
7. Pictures 23, 24, and 25 *or* 27, 28, and 29 call for the use of the verbs *walk, eat,* and *ride* or equivalent expressions. ("Food" may be substituted for *eat* and "boat" for *ride,* but there is no easy substitute for *walk.*)
8. Pictures 2, 4, and 41 *or* 6, 8, and 42 call for the use of *nobody, no one, nothing* or equivalent expressions.

Level II-A: Games To Teach Two-Term Constructions

1. Photographs 1, 2, 3, and 4 *or* 5, 6, 7, and 8 call for the use of agent-object constructions.
2. Photographs 23, 24, 25, 27, 28, and 29 call for agent-action or agent-object constructions.
3. Photographs 2, 4, 15, and 17 call for agent-action constructions.
4. Photographs 41, 42, 43, and 44 call for modifier-noun constructions.

Level III-A: Games To Teach Multiword Constructions and Modulations

1. Photographs 1, 2, 3, 4, 5, 6, 7, and 8 call for agent-modifier-object constructions.
2. Photographs 2, 4, 9, 10, 12, and 13 call for agent-action-object constructions.
3. Photographs 31, 32, 33, and 34 teach contrastive word order.
4. Photographs 35, 36, 37, and 38 *or* 35, 36, 37, 38, 39, and 40 call for complicated agent-action-modifier-object constructions plus the expression *each other.*
5. Photographs 25, 26, 29, and 30 require that both the agent and the object be modified by a color term.
6. Photographs 2, 4, 6, 8, 41, and 42 call for agent-modifier (-object) constructions using *nobody, no one* or equivalent expressions.

Communicative Bingo and Lotto
(Chapter 6)

The same sets of pictures used for the Hiding Games with Pictures above can be used for Lotto or Bingo. The photographs are arranged in front of the listener. The speaker has a duplicate set of the pictures and tells the listener which photograph to cover with a poker chip (Bingo) or which to point to (Lotto).

A complicated Bingo or Lotto game can be made from pictures 2, 4, 6, 8, 10, 11, 13, 14, 15, 16, 17, 18, 19, 20, 21, and 22.

Picture-Toy Matching Games
(Chapter 7)

The speaker has a subset of the photographs, and the listener has the toys shown in the photographs. The speaker draws one photograph and tells the listener how to arrange the toys so that they look exactly the way they do in the photograph. When the listener has arranged the toys, the speaker displays the photograph, and the players check the match between the photograph and toys. The sets of pictures selected for use at Levels I, II, and III are the same as those listed for Hiding Games. As a child masters a set of pictures, a new set can gradually be introduced so that the child is working with a large set of the photographs. The following sets could be used to prepare the child gradually to work with the entire deck of photographs:

1. photographs 1, 6, 9, 16, and 20
2. photographs 1, 2, 9, 10, 11, 15, and 19
3. photographs 37, 38, 39, and 40
4. photographs 23, 24, 25, 26, 27, 28, 29, and 30
5. photographs 1, 3, 5, 7, 9, 12, 23, 24, 25, 26, 27, 28, 29, and 30

Identical Arrangement Games
(Chapter 8)

Each player has an identical subset of the toys, and the players are separated by a screen. The speaker arranges his toys, then tells the listener how to duplicate that arrangement. Initially, each player may have only a small subset of the toys. One new element may then be introduced at a time. Examples of small subsets follow:

1. Superman, the black dinosaur, and the red boat
2. the Hulk, the black dinosaur, and the red boat
3. Superman, the black dinosaur, and the red dinosaur
4. the Hulk, the black dinosaur, and the red dinosaur
5. the black dinosaur, the red dinosaur, and the food

Guess and Keep (Chapter 10)

This game is appropriate for children who have played extensively with the photographs. A subset of the photographs is placed face down on the playing surface. The speaker points to one photograph and guesses which one it is. If he guesses correctly, he keeps the picture. The other player becomes the speaker, and the process continues. At the end, the players may count up to see who has more photographs, but this competitive element is optional.

Hiding Games with Objects (Chapter 5)

"Who Has...?" (Level I-A)

This game is used to elicit the names of other players, who are concealing toys. It may be played with:

1. the Superman doll
2. the Hulk doll
3. the red dinosaur toy
4. the black dinosaur toy

The game might also be played with a photograph of one of these toys to introduce children to the photographs. (The photograph would be a substitute for the small object hidden.)

Practical Notes

Toy Selection

The selection of toys for the communication games is governed first by the same principles that apply to any selection of toys for young children and second by considerations unique to the communication games.

Any toys to be used by young children must, above all else, be safe. Young children mouth toys, drop and then mouth them, and are otherwise likely to swallow bits of paint and small parts. Any toy intended for young children should be "childproofed" by a destruction-bent adult before the child ever sees the toy. The wise adult drops the toys, yanks at small parts, bends parts that look breakable, and otherwise tries to discover the hidden hazards of a toy. Any toy failing this test should not be used in the games. The paint on all toys should be nontoxic.

Toys should also be durable. A toy that lasts only until a child uses it is useless. Simple toys tend to be the most successful. A toy with many small parts and complicated workings is apt to be both unsafe and easily ruined. Small parts get lost. Simple toys are also best in the communication games because complex toys often pose imposssible challenges when the children must describe them. A red truck is generally better than a red and black truck with yellow swirls on its sides. A plain black dinosaur is apt to be more useful than a multicolored dinosaur.

While adults often like wooden toys with a natural finish, children usually go for flashy toys. A bright red fire engine with gleaming chrome appeals to the average child much more than a natural wood truck intended to stimulate his imagination. A fancy-looking doll in a gaudy dress is apt to be much more appealing to a child than the simple rag doll an adult would prefer. Unhappily, few toys are durable and simple, yet flashy.

Toys should also be realistic in the sense that toys intended to be miniatures should look as much as possible like the full-scale versions. A little fire truck is easy to recognize as a fire truck if it really looks like a tiny version of a genuine one. Unfortunately, miniature versions of refrigerators, stoves, bathtubs, and such are often available only in unlikely colors and without appropriate detail. Highly realistic versions of furniture and vehicles are often available only in very expensive sets intended for adult-owned dollhouses. Whenever possible, however, a more realistic toy is generally a better choice than a less realistic one.

The dolls and toy animals for the games are most useful if they are poseable. Dolls with bendable knees, rubber animals that can assume many stances, and other figures that move are useful in making these characters ride in vehicles, sit realistically, hold things, and otherwise illustrate actions and events. A sometimes conflicting requirement is that the figures be easy to manipulate. The easiest figures for children to place in chairs, vehicles, and such are nonposeable ones. In particular, peg dolls are very easy to place in the little cars, playpens, rocking horses, and other items that are available for peg dolls. Some sets of interesting and highly poseable dolls are extremely difficult to manipulate. For example, dolls with special "hands" for grasping things are useless for very young children and for older children with fine motor problems. Acrobat dolls that grasp the bars of miniature gymnastics sets, motorcycle riders that stand upside down on the bars of the cycles, and other such flashy and appealing toys performing interesting actions are usually impossible for children to manipulate.

In our search for appropriate figures, we have sometimes come across poseable dolls that are inappropriate because they are grotesque. Bendable rubber dolls of human figures often seem to be frightening caricatures and should be avoided. Badly designed rubber animals, however, have a particular use in communicative work. A small orange animal that could be a sheep, monkey, or dog is useful because there is genuine uncertainty about what it is. The adult faced with such a toy can honestly ask the child, *What's that?*, without already knowing the answer.

The selection of toys for the games is guided as well by their potential for systematic variation. For example, dinosaurs that come in four distinctly different colors are potentially useful in one-word color games and in two-word games in which different characters ride on different dinosaurs. A lone multicolored dinosaur does not have this potential. A set of superhero dolls that do not look like one another has more potential in the games than a single superhero doll, however attractive. Two dolls representing motorcycle riders wearing jackets of different colors, together with two motorcycles that also differ in color, have potential for many games: The man in the red jacket can ride the green motorcycle or the blue motorcycle, as can the man in the yellow jacket. Either rider can fall off either cycle. One rider and one cycle have few possibilities, and riders difficult to describe lack potential.

The selection of toys, in short, generally involves hours of hunting through toy stores and five-and-dime stores. Fortunately, most schools have many toys that can be used in communication games not requiring duplicate sets of toys. For example, peg doll sets of nursery and *Sesame Street* characters can be photographed and used in Picture-Toy Matching Games.

Pictures

Three kinds of pictures may be used in Hiding and Lotto Games: drawings, commercially available photographs, and photographs taken especially for the games.

Drawings, especially line drawings, require considerable interpretation. Many special-needs children have observable difficulty understanding the conventions of pictorial representation. A line drawing intended to represent a house, a cat, a plane, or another object may be a meaningless scribble to the child. Alternatively, it may convey some meaning other than that intended. These problems of interpretation are especially noticeable when the drawings are intended to represent general or abstract concepts: school, teacher, mother, and so forth. A line drawing of a woman standing next to a blackboard, perhaps holding a pointer, bears no relationship to a preschool child's experience with teachers. The child may not even understand that the drawing represents a person or a school. In teaching words like *teacher*, then, it is better to use photographs, and better still to use photographs of the child's own teacher.

There are, however, occasions when it is appropriate to use drawings. Some commercially available games and language materials may be adapted for use in a communication game. For example, sets of Lotto are available with drawings of familiar objects like dogs, horses, and trucks. Some sets of picture cards show the same character in different locations (e.g., a cat in, on, and under a box). Pictures are suitable if the children for whom a game is intended have no trouble interpreting them. In general, the less stylized the drawings, the better.

Drawings are particularly useful in the communication games to show Santa Claus, Snoopy, *Sesame Street* characters, and other characters and events children frequently experience as drawings. Snoopy, for instance, *is* a cartoon character. Consequently, games about Snoopy show conventional representations of Snoopy. In constructing games about characters like Snoopy, Santa Claus, and such, it is easy and convenient to use booklets or sheets of stickers that are widely and inexpensively available. These stickers may be placed on 3-by-5 cards or on other backing, laminated, and used as pictures.

Commercially available photographs, including photographs from language development kits and photographs from magazines, are sometimes useful. One problem with using these photographs is that they frequently contain irrelevant and distracting material. For example, if one wants a picture of a horse, it may be difficult to find a photograph showing a horse but not people or animals. A second problem occurs when one needs a set of pictures that vary systematically in certain ways: a cat on a chair, the same cat under a chair, a dog on a chair, and the same dog under a chair. Commercially available pictures are seldom available in sets like these.

Photographs taken especially for the games have many advantages over drawings and commercially available photographs. They may be pictures of the children themselves; these pictures have an obvious motivational value. They may be pictures of people, places, and objects familiar to the children. Fortunately, taking these photographs does not require any particular expertise. Instant cameras are easy to use and produce clear, sharp pictures durable enough to withstand repeated handling by children. These photographs do not require laminating and can be wiped clean.

Lotto Game Construction

Lotto Games deserve considerable care in construction mainly because various elements of the game materials for Lotto may be used to play other games as well. The pictures from Lotto Games may all be used in Hiding Games. Photographs used for Lotto are also used in some Picture-Toy Matching Games. The pictures for complex Lotto Games may form subsets for simple vocabulary Lotto Games. Because the pictures for Lotto frequently are multipurpose and take a hard beating with repeated use, it is important to construct these games so that they are durable and effective.

Because Lotto materials must exist in duplicate, pictures cut from magazines, photographs from traditional language development kits, and other materials difficult to locate in duplicate are seldom appropriate. It is occasionally possible to use duplicate sets of language development materials. Pictures appropriate for two-word and multiword Lotto Games are practically never available in magazines or traditional kits. One seldom comes across photographs of the same cat on and under the same box and the same dog on and under the same box.

The photographs taken for Lotto Games must be clear, sharp, uncluttered depictions of the objects, actions, or other features of interest. If a picture is intended to show one child drinking from a water fountain, the child should be alone, should not be holding a toy, and should not be doing anything else. The fewer distractions in the picture, the better. Keeping pictures simple and uncluttered is more important for communication games than for other kinds of language development activities because of the purpose for which the pictures are used. If the child can describe a picture effectively by naming some distracting object in it, then the child has communicated effectively. *Teddy bear* may be an adequate description of a picture that shows a child drinking from a water fountain while holding a teddy bear. Similarly, the objects depicted must be clear. A fuzzy and unrecognizable picture of another child is useless. Photographs intended to show colors must show those colors perfectly. A red car must be red.

Redundancy helps direct the child's attention to certain features of the photographs. For instance, pictures of various animals eating and drinking foods should show the containers of food as well as the dishes. *Milk* should be a glass or bowl of milk next to a carton of a popular brand of milk. *Ice cream* should be a dish of ice cream next to a large carton with a picture of a big dish of the same flavor of ice cream.

Instant photographs have some advantages over ordinary snapshots. First, there is no waiting time involved. If one realizes that a particular game would be helpful to a child, one may make materials for the game immediately. Second, these photographs are very durable and easy to clean. They require no backing or lamination. Third, children can participate in the making of games from instant pictures. On the other hand, however, instant photographs are very expensive.

Stickers are also useful. To create two-word games, it is necessary to have a variety of stickers from which to pick. For instance, various stickers showing Santa Claus trimming a Christmas tree, children trimming a Christmas tree, a candy cane on a Christmas tree, a candy cane in a stocking, and so forth are needed. To obtain these combinations, it is usually necessary to buy as many different brands of stickers as possible. Rather than buying one package of bird stickers, one of animal stickers, one of Christmas stickers, and so forth, one must buy five or six different booklets on each theme.

One way to use stickers to make the games is to create combinations by cutting off selected portions of stickers. For example, if a sticker shows a cat sitting on a pillow, one may cut the pillow off one pair of cat stickers but leave another pair intact. This kind of alteration of the stickers is sometimes helpful. Different brands of stickers sometimes yield combinations (e.g., an elephant with its trunk up in the air, another elephant with its trunk down; a smiling pumpkin and a frowning pumpkin; a pumpkin with a hat, a pumpkin with no hat). Because the greatest variety of brands is usually available in stickers with holiday themes, Halloween, Christmas, Valentine's Day, and other holiday games can easily be made from stickers. Furthermore, holiday characters and objects are generally known to children mainly in the form of drawings, so the interpretation of the drawings is not a major problem.

When stickers are used to make Lotto Games, it is necessary to put the stickers on heavy backing and laminate the pictures. Ordinary 3-by-5 file cards are a suitable backing. Regardless of whether stickers, photographs, or commercially available materials are used, it is important that the resulting pictures be large enough for the children to handle easily.

Pilot Testing

Before investing a great deal of effort in the construction of a large and complicated Lotto Game, one should try out an initial version of the materials. Pictures sometimes convey meanings other than those intended. Details that seem irrelevant to adults are sometimes salient for children. Childen are sometimes misled by pictures that seem clear to adults. Before laminating a set of materials, it is a good idea to use the materials briefly with a child who is unlikely to damage them.

A particularly easy way to test materials for Lotto is to make only one set and to use that set in a Hiding Game. If the pictures are interesting and meaningful to the children in that format, they can then be duplicated for use in Lotto.

Master Cards vs. Arrays

Commercially available sets of Lotto consist of master cards, usually with about six or eight pictures per card, plus matching single-picture calling cards. For the purposes of the communication games, it is not necessary to fasten pictures onto permanent master cards, and there are several reasons to avoid doing so. Once a set of pictures is permanently fastened onto a master card, a game is fixed. For example, in a color Lotto Game, once a master card has four color chips on it, one cannot easily transform it into a master card containing those four colors and one more color. Similarly, if the four colors are clearly too difficult for a child to manage, one cannot easily change the card so that it has only two or three colors. It is possible, of course, to make all of the master cards one might ever need for every set of materials, but this undertaking involves making dozens of sets of master cards even for a very simple game with a few basic elements. Furthermore, when the pictures used in the game are photographs, the cost of having many reproductions made is very high.

Consequently, communicative Lotto and Bingo Games usually consist of multiple sets of pictures that can be arrayed in front of children and simplified and elaborated as needed. If the pictures are not permanently fastened onto master cards, the same set of materials can be used for many children with different needs, and the games can be made gradually more complicated as the child masters them.

Summary

One detailed example described the design of Level I, II, and III games, and a second illustrated the process of planning and constructing a game. A third example provided specific details about one large set of materials for playing a variety of games in different formats.

The selection of toys for the games is governed by the same principles that apply to any selection of toys for young children (e.g., safety, durability, simplicity, and appeal) and by considerations unique to the games (e.g., potential for systematic controlled variation). Drawings, commercially available photographs, and photographs taken especially for the games are useful for different purposes.

13
Conducting a Session

The issues discussed in this chapter are not specific to this language program. Any skilled therapist, teacher, or parent is familiar with strategies for helping children make transitions from one activity to another, for helping children control their behavior, and for pacing and timing activities. Furthermore, the particular way in which language intervention sessions are conducted is a function of the context in which they are conducted. A parent working in the context of the home faces problems that a teacher does not encounter, while a teacher faces problems that a parent does not encounter. In explaining how to conduct sessions, then, we are not setting down fixed rules about one and only one way to use the communication games. Rather, we are suggesting some strategies that should be modified according to the setting in which one works.

Preparing a Space

Before beginning a session, it is imperative to have a work space defined and arranged. Regardless of whether this space is a corner of the classroom, a small room, or a kitchen table, the space should be uncluttered. The space should be

defined and relatively constant. The child should be able to predict where he
will play the games and should know where to stay during the playing. In very
distracting surroundings, it is helpful to use a rug or several small mats to
define the space.

The only game materials or toys available should be those the child is to
use. The remaining materials should be available to the adult but not to the
child.

Greeting and Preparing the Child

A parent or classroom teacher may prepare the child to play by telling him
that he will have a chance to play that day. The speech therapist or special-
needs teacher who must work with the children outside the classroom or in a
special part of the classroom usually needs to do more elaborate preparation.
While some children are always eager for "special time" with an adult, other
children are extremely reluctant to change activities. In particular, a
language-disabled child who is resistant to talking or who has a history of
failure in situations requiring talk may be very hesitant.

The worst possible way to approach a reluctant child is to march up and
ask, "Would you like to go with me now?". The resistant child usually ignores
the question or conveys a negative response. Rather, one first greets the child.
It may be helpful to do this when one first arrives at the school, long before the
child will actually be expected to leave the classroom or to change activities. At
that time, one makes a simple statement to the effect that the child will have a
turn to play that day. When dealing with a reluctant child, it is usually a
mistake to phrase this statement as an interrogative. Say, "We'll have a chance
to play later.", not "Would you like to play later?". The most effective way to
elicit the child's cooperation is to assume that the child will play. It may be
helpful to notice one's own intonation and pitch when saying, for example,
"The sun will rise tomorrow." That is the correct way to say "You'll have a
turn."

Occasionally, a child is hesitant to enter situations unless he has control
over the entrance and timing. In that case, it may be helpful to ask a child
whether he wants to play now or later. Again, however, one must convey
clearly the idea that the session will take place.

Children who must leave the classroom for special-needs activities
sometimes have valid, important reasons for wanting to stay in the room.
They do not want to miss interesting events. It is tactless to insist that a child
leave the room while all of the other children are about to begin an interesting

project. It may be important to reassure a child that he will be back in time to have snack, to make a collage, or to do other things.

Indirect approaches are sometimes effective. It may help a child to make the transition from the classroom to the games if he has something else to think about. Start a conversation. Talk about a new toy. Admire the child's T-shirt. Casually take the child's hand, tell him it's time to play, then keep on talking as you leave the room.

Another way to facilitate the transition is to help the child gain closure on whatever he has been doing. If the child is playing with blocks that might be put away, help the child put away the blocks. Explain that as soon as the blocks have been put away, you will be able to play. Write the child's name on a picture he is finishing. Let him watch a favorite television show until it ends. Wait for a natural transition period in the classroom schedule. Help the child find a way to finish the activity so that he will be psychologically ready to begin something else.

Serious Problems

The communication games are very appealing, and one encounters few problems in persuading children to play. If a serious problem arises, it is important to examine frankly one's own conduct with the child. Is the child playing the games in an arrangement of players that he or she enjoys? A child may be reluctant to play with one adult but happy to play with his friend Billy. If so, invite Billy to play. Is the child experiencing a sense of incompetence in the games? If so, play games in which the child can experience success. No manipulative effort or trick is as effective in making a child eager to play as providing an activity so interesting that the child cannot resist.

Find out what the child likes and do it. One therapist who experienced repeated frustration in trying to persuade a reluctant child to leave the room discovered that the child loved the music from the show *Annie*. The therapist made a tape recording of songs from *Annie*, and she and the child began every session by singing *Tomorrow* together.

Two issues sometimes complicate the adult's facility in helping a child to make the transition to the games. First, adults who overvalue obedience may lose sight of their purpose in interacting with the child. The point of the games is to help children communicate, not to make them obedient. A child who yells, "No, I don't want to play." is a child using words to communicate. One finds a way to help the child play; one does not take umbrage at the child's sentiment. Second, adults sometimes blame the child or someone else for the child's reluctance. If only someone else did not drag the child out of the room,

if only the child were less diffusely angry, if only something were different—
then one would not be responsible. In fact, there are events beyond one's
control that make some children hesitant. It is important not to take the
child's reluctance too personally. On the other hand, the child is still one's
responsiblity. An adult involved in this kind of difficult situation needs
outside help. Find out how others handle the child. Ask a supervisor for
advice. Know when to give up for the day. It is always counterproductive to
create a scene in which the adult forces an unwilling child to play. When one
feels that this is the only available option, one should give up for the day.

Advantages of the Classroom

Working in the child's classroom minimizes these problems in making the
transition to playing the games. The child can see that he is not missing
anything new and wonderful. The hesitant child can see others playing. The
very hesitant child may be encouraged to wander over to the playing area and
to hang around watching others having fun.

Beginning and Conducting a Session

Having brought the child to the playing space, one need not instantly begin a
game. The child may need a little time to warm up. The adult may start a
general conversation at a level appropriate to the child. The adult may show
the child a new game and let the child play with the materials.

Some children enjoy choosing which game to play first. The adult may
show the child several sets of materials and let the child select one set. Children
sometimes request particular games spontaneously. If the child is too
unfamiliar with the games to make a choice or unable to deal with the freedom
of choosing a game, the adult should use several guidelines to select the first
game. In general, the sequence of games played in one session goes from easy
to difficult and from new to old. A new game gets a session off to a lively start.
A rather dull game, one that the child has played many times or one that the
child does not particularly enjoy, should be sandwiched between other games.
If the last game is particularly difficult, it might be followed by a very brief
period of playing an easy game. In other words, the playing should begin and
end with the child experiencing success.

There are no rules about how many different games to use in a session. The
number of games is determined, in part, by the length of a session, as discussed
below. Children working on complicated theme games may devote a long

session to one game. Children with very short attention spans may move rapidly from one game to another. If the adult wants such a child to work intensively on some particular content, all of these different games might involve the same concept. For example, six different games all involving *on* and *under* might be used one right after the other.

Length of Sessions

How long any session should last is determined by the child's capacity to attend to the games. In general, a session should end a few minutes *before* the child is satiated. A session has lasted too long if the child begins to shuffle and squirm, announces that he doesn't want to play anymore, or looks imploringly and asks, "Room?". The length of sessions may vary with the child's level of intellectual functioning. A very bright child may be able to play a series of different games that holds his attention for a long time. Some children show marked day-to-day fluctuations. In a lively, cheerful mood a child may play for half an hour, while in a morose mood the same child may tire after ten minutes. Our experience is that about 45 minutes is the longest session any young child can tolerate with interest.

When working in a school, it is important to consider the needs of other people who work with the child. If a child is scheduled to have another individual session with another special-needs teacher, the child should have some energy left for that work. It is also important to consider the child's classroom schedule. In particular, if a child has been assured that he will not miss snack or music, it is important to keep that promise. This timing is also important at home; a child who has been promised that he will not miss *Sesame Street* should not miss it.

Children's Behavior

Sessions go smoothly if children clearly understand the basic rules of behavior appropriate to the situation. Some children never present any behavior problems at all. Others test limits at every session. In school settings, one must maintain continuity with the school. If the school forbids running in the halls, it is unwise to permit the children to run through the halls. In enforcing rules like this, positive statements work more effectively than criticism. It is helpful to praise the child for walking while he is walking. It is also helpful to present rules as flat descriptions including everyone, not just the child: "*We* walk in the hall. *We* don't run."

Another useful device is the old trick of passing the buck. Instead of issuing an order as a personal command, one implicates others as the source of the rule: "When we are in school, *people* like us to *walk* in the hall. They don't like us to run." This phrasing is much more acceptable to most children than a personal directive, like "I want you to walk." Praising other children's admirable behavior sometimes has a positive effect on the behavior of observing children. For example, "Mary, you're walking through the hall just like a first grader." may help another child shape up.

When behavior problems arise during sessions, it is sometimes a signal that a change in the arrangement of players, the games, or the timing is needed. Two children may encourage one another's wild behavior. A child may find a game too challenging and may avoid playing it by throwing toys. A session may have lasted too long for the child to tolerate. When a child misbehaves during a session, the child should be told immediately that "This is how we play." and "This is how we don't play." Sometimes it is helpful simply to state flatly, "No throwing toys." If simple limit-setting does not work, the session should be ended immediately.

When enforcing rules or ending sessions because of misbehavior, it is important to give dull responses to the misbehavior. The session ended because of misbehavior should end in a maximally uninteresting way. The child should not have evidence that the misbehavior interested the adult. As little as possible should happen. The child should be encouraged to conclude that the misbehavior was no fun.

Ending a Session

Approximately two-thirds of the way through the session, the child should be warned that the end of the session is approaching (e.g., *Not too much time left. Pretty soon we'll go back to your room. It'll be snack time pretty soon.*). Another announcement of the impending end should be given near the end (e.g., *When we're done with this.... Only one more turn.*).

Children may be helped to anticipate the transition back to other activities if they have something specific to anticipate. If the child will return to snack time, the adult may announce that and may start a conversation about snacks. Picking up and putting away the game materials may help children finish the session psychologically. Some children enjoy a ritual of saying good-bye. Other rituals may be devised as well.

In returning a child to the classroom, it is important not to disrupt the ongoing activities of the class. If the room has several doors, one door may be more distant from centers of activity than another. A child may enter the room more smoothly if one walks him in and makes sure that he becomes engaged in an activity. Teachers may have strong preferences about how children are returned and should be asked about their preferences.

Summary

The smooth conduct of sessions is facilitated by defining the game-playing space and by preparing the children for the transition to the game. During the playing, the usual sequence of games is from easy to difficult and from old to new games, with the final game always one in which the child experiences success. The number of different games played and the length of sessions vary from child to child. Behavior problems are avoided by making the rules for behavior clear; by changing playing arrangements, games, and timing; and by making sure that misbehavior has boring consequences. The transition from the games to other activities is facilitated by telling the child in advance that the session will end soon, by helping the child anticipate the activities that will follow, and by providing transitional rituals.

14
The Transition To Communicative Teaching: Impediments and Tactics

Making the transition from a traditional to a communicative approach to early childhood language intervention involves changes in teaching priorities, in specific methods, and in the ideal image of the learning situation one wants to create. The communicative approach differs from the traditional approach in emphasizing articulation, vocabulary, and grammar only as they affect the child's success in communicating with other people. The teaching methods, not just the goals, are communicative: The communicative therapist or teacher avoids any pointless or arbitrary demands and rewards for talking and creates real, if playful, reasons to talk. The ideal image of the learning situation is one involving genuine two-way exchanges of information.

The transition from a traditional to a communicative approach, in short, involves a pervasive change in the practitioner's interaction with young children in structured and unstructured settings. Because this change is a radical one, it seldom occurs smoothly and easily. The purpose of this chapter is to describe common problems that characterize and impede the transition and to suggest some steps toward solving those problems.

Arbitrary Demands

The single most common problem practitioners have in using the communication games is using them as a generalization activity rather than as a teaching method. The most common manifestation of this problem occurs at the very beginning of a playing session. The practitioner selects the materials for a game, shows the materials to the children, then asks the children to label the materials: "What's this? Do you know what this is? What is the boy doing?" If the children correctly supply the labels, the practitioner concludes that the children are ready to play the game. If the children fail to produce the labels, the practitioner concludes that the children are not yet ready for this game.

Seibert and Oller (1981) describe as "pragmatically counter-productive...the procedure of holding up a single desired object and demanding the label, either imitatively or in response to 'What's this?' or 'What do you want?' Such a situation clearly violates the rules for sincerity and naturalness in normal communicative interaction, since (a) the adult already knows the name of the object, (b) the adult already knows that the child wants the object, and (c) the child is aware of all this. The end result of such a procedure may either be a compliant child who gives responses on command but may be hesitant to communicate his/her needs to such an adult, or a continuous power struggle between adult and child over who is controlling whom. Neither outcome seems conducive to communication development." (p. 83)

Requests for pointless labeling are a common example of a general class of pointless demands: demands for exact repetitions of adult model sentences, for perfect articulation, and for other responses designed to please rather than to inform adults. Test questions or known-information questions are questions like *How many blocks are here?*, *What day is today?* and *What did Peter Rabbit do then?* These kinds of devices serve one positive function: They permit adults to set children up to display competence with language. They trigger competent children to perform well. Unhappily, they practically never serve that function with language-disabled children; rather, they serve as a means of reinforcing everyone's experience of the child as disabled and incompetent.

Solutions

The easiest way to break oneself of the habit of eliciting labels and otherwise prefacing and punctuating the games with noncommunicative training efforts is to eradicate from one's vocabulary all the usual formulas for eliciting labels. In short, forbid oneself *What's this?*, *Who is that?*, *What is he doing?*, *What color is this?*, *This is a....*, and all other such formulas.

It may be helpful to provide oneself with a substitute activity, such as performing the labeling oneself. In introducing the game materials, one may casually describe them: "Today we're going to play with pictures of Billy and Mike. Here's a picture of Mike...." It is best to avoid an artificial and stilted manner when giving these descriptions. To say loudly, slowly, or ponderously, "THIS (pause) IS (pause) A BUNNY RABBIT." is to spoil the conversational tone of the playing situation. A model to bear in mind is one's own verbal behavior in casual situations: "Hmm, tuna fish sandwiches, fried chicken, iced tea." The tone appropriate for providing a verbal survey of a picnic is the tone appropriate for surveying the game materials. In any case, if one feels a need to have someone label the game materials, one performs that act oneself. One does not extract labels from the children.

The communication games provide a structure that helps the adult avoid test questions; the games place the adult in the uninformed role of listener as well as in the informed role of speaker. In interactions outside the games, however, the transition from known-information questions and arbitrary demands to other kinds of speech acts may be a difficult one. The adult who works with severely disabled preschoolers may initially wonder: What can I possibly ask that this child knows and I don't? In fact, the adult has no direct line to the child's intentions and does not observe the child outside the classroom. Both of these areas provide plentiful material. As adults, we do not necessarily know what children want and think. We do not know what colors they prefer in crayons, what kind of snack they like, whether they want to wash their hands at a particular moment. We do not always know what they do at home. What happened on *Sesame Street*? Have the children watched particular situation comedies? Have they gone to McDonalds with their families? These kinds of topics interest children more and provide them with more to say than questions about what day it is and what labels are used for objects we are well able to label ourselves.

Listener Tactics

A more general line of attack on the problem of making arbitrary demands is to place oneself firmly in the role of listener and to develop tactics for becoming the kind of listener who effectively transforms the child into an active speaker.

The listener, by definition, lacks information needed to play. Ideally, the only source of that information is what the speaker says. In reality, the adult listener often has the option of gaining the information either by shrewd guessing or by visual transmission. Adults can see over screens designed for children. Children inadvertently or deliberately leak information.

Ignorance Tactics

Listener tactics include tactics for maintaining one's genuine ignorance. The most effective way to do this is to avoid looking at the potential source of leaked information by staring fixedly at one's own game materials and not gazing in the area where the child is apt to display his. This refusal to look is usually more effective than repeatedly telling the child not to show things.

Whenever possible, it is best to remain ignorant of the key material the child is supposed to convey. If one is inadvertently informed, however, it is possible to feign ignorance. Feigning ignorance is best avoided with older or more capable children; with these children it may be tantamount to crying wolf. The children may lose the sense that the listener really does need to have the information verbalized. In contrast, children functioning at a very low cognitive level may have great difficulty understanding whether one is really informed; feigning ignorance may be necessary to keep the game moving.

An ignorance tactic occasionally useful in work with children functioning at a very low level is to act as if one had been adequately informed by the child's words when, in fact, one gained the needed information elsewhere. This tactic is mainly useful when a child seems to have no faith in his power to communicate with people by using words. Suppose that a child hardly ever talks. The few words he produces as the speaker are poorly articulated. In a game, he manages to produce a sound that seems to be an approximation of some word. The adult happens to have glimpsed the picture the child is using and knows that the child is probably trying to say *milk*. In this situation, it is advisable to act as if the child's effort to verbalize had actually been informative. In later work, as the child progresses, one may do what behaviorists aptly call "upping the ante"; one may raise one's standards for what counts as a correct response. In the communication games, the equivalent process is to begin to feign ignorance or to keep oneself genuinely ignorant so that one really does come to depend upon the child's words for the information.

Restating

The adult in the role of listener has available a range of tactics for eliciting or facilitating the speaker's talk. One of the most common is repetition in any of its many forms. As Persson (1974) discusses, repetition is an extremely complex phenomenon. One may echo another, restate meaning, restate one word but not others, echo another's syntax but not particular words, and so forth.

The adult listener who restates the child speaker's message says aloud, as if to himself, whatever the child said (or evidently meant). In so doing, the adult provides the child with a clear model and with the chance to give corrective feedback. In addition, he implicitly assures the child that what the child intended to say was successfully transmitted. Because one function of repetition is modeling, it is best to avoid repeating errors of articulation or syntax. To do so would also be to risk embarrassing the child. Repetition in this context may, however, include expanding and/or extending children's utterances. If the child produces a two-word utterance, one may repeat it as a fully formed sentence. For example, if the child provides the adequate but telegraphic utterance "Man sit.", the adult may say, "Hm, the man is sitting."

A rather complex form of repetition is useful in elaborate games: The adult listener, besides using repetition to provide a model of sentences, to invite feedback, and to assure the child of information transmission, also repeats to impose a structure on the child's successive utterances. In this kind of modeling, the adult shows the child how to use words to paint a whole picture. In effect, the adult provides a model of how to turn sentences into paragraphs as well as a model of how to link words together into sentences. Complex modeling is particularly appropriate in games that have a potential narrative structure, such as Narrative Hiding Games, Identical Arrangement Games played with sets of toys, and Identical Arrangement Games played with sequential picture cards.

Listing Possibilities

If a child speaker appears to be stuck, two tactics are useful. First, one may ask yes-no questions (e.g., *Is it the blue one? Is he on the truck?*). Second, one may list some or all possibilities (e.g., *The cat, the dog, or the horse?*). The major advantage of the second tactic is the provision of a model of what to say. This tactic is often useful in work with children who have word-finding problems. Having been reminded of a word, the child may be able to formulate a long and communicatively adequate utterance. Notice that these tactics have the advantage of naturalness; ordinary conversation with children frequently involves adults in exactly this kind of prompting.

Feeding Echolalia

The listing of alternatives is also useful in a maneuver effective with echolalic children and children who simply use repetition as a language-learning strategy. With these children, one's aim is to make constructive use of the echolalia or repetition by maneuvering the child into a position in which the repetition has communicative consequences. Stating one alternative or listing alternatives is the first step in this maneuver. One feeds the echolalia, so to speak, by repeatedly saying what one hopes the child will say (e.g., *The cat? Which one? The kitty-cat? The cat?*). With a little luck the child provides the second step by repeating the key word or phrase: "Cat." The third step is to treat that repetition communicatively, to embed it in a meaningful context by treating it as a message intended to provide information (e.g., *Cat? Yes, I have a cat. Let's look there.*).

Words and Uses

The tenacity of the habit of eliciting labels is perhaps best understood in the context of experiences that adults and children have in the academic learning of vocabulary — that is, in the context of what might be called the *Reader's Digest* model of language learning. First one learns a list of words, then one learns to use the words.

In contrast to the learn-it-then-use-it model, the model underlying the communicative approach rejects the distinction between learning words and learning uses. In this model, as Wittgenstein (1969) writes, "a meaning of a word is a kind of employment of it" (p. 10). Learning to comprehend and produce words *is* learning to use them to understand others and to express oneself.

Monopolizing the Speaker Role

A second common problem in using the communication games is monopolizing the role of the speaker. The practitioner with this problem has no difficulty beginning a game. He or she starts the play but never moves beyond the beginning. The child begins in the listener role and remains there. The practitioner with this problem often says that the child is not ready for the speaker role. This explanation is so frequent that it may be helpful in identifying this problem in one's own teaching.

A second signal that one may be experiencing this problem is a tendency to call the speaker role the "teacher" role. This labeling clearly stems from a traditional conception of who the teacher is: the active person who tells other people what to do and who has information unavailable to others. The teacher who wants to fill the role of teacher must, then, remain the speaker. In the communication games — and in conversational intervention in general — the most difficult teaching task is to help the children become active people who communicate new information to other people. Monopolizing the speaker role is hence counterproductive. One's goal is to abandon that role to the children, not to cling to it.

Solution

The solution to the problem of monopolizing the speaker role is to institute a rigid rule that one *always* reverses roles at each round of a game. The practitioner who shows no tendency to monopolize the speaker role may be flexible about role reversal. The practitioner with this tendency needs to be rigid until his or her own impulse to monopolize the speaker role is under control.

In itself, calling the speaker role the teacher role is not a problem. Children as well as practitioners sometimes refer to the speaker as the teacher. Children often enjoy being told that they are now the teachers. When the children and the teacher all have turns as teacher, no one has a monopoly, and the terminology itself creates no impediment to the playing process.

Monopolizing Central Roles

Practitioners sometimes successfully avoid monopolizing any one role yet encounter a new problem: always retaining a central role. In particular, they act as switchboards in mediating all communication. This problem is evident when one practitioner works with two or more children. As a result, the interaction follows only one pattern: adult-child-adult-child. In contrast, communicative work aims to achieve an idealized state in which the adult is superfluous, or has the option to participate or not. The more the adult can turn over the central roles to the children, the better.

An extreme form of adult overmediation occurs when the practitioner engages in one-to-one work in the context of a small group. For example, a teacher is working with two children using an Identical Arrangement Game. The adult gives one set of toys to one child and keeps another set. The adult places the screen between himself and the child with the toys. He then plays the role of speaker, instructing the child with the toys to arrange them in some way. He removes the screen, and the adult and child compare the arrangements. That child then becomes the speaker while the adult becomes the listener in a new round. What happens to the second child? Observation suggests that the second child does not cooperatively wait, listen and learn from competent models, and otherwise glean benefit from this chance to be a spectator. Rather, he fidgets, yawns, sighs, and eventually finds some annoying way to gain the adult's attention. Indeed, young children loathe the role of spectator and are adept at finding ways to step out of it.

Solution

The solution to the problem is probably obvious. Adults are capable spectators, while children are not. The adult needs to exchange roles with the excluded child. The screen belongs between the two children, and the two sets of toys belong in front of the children.

The underlying impediment to structuring interaction between the children now emerges. What is left for the adult to do? How can the teacher teach without monopolizing a central role? There is seldom a shortage of roles for the teacher to play. He may share a role with the less able of the two children. He may join with one of the children so that the two play as a unit. If the two children are reasonably competent players, he may be most helpful by fighting the urge to talk while the children work things out for themselves. In any case, the adult will not be derelict as a teacher simply because he is the spectator.

Short-Circuiting Communication Failure

The practitioner who short-circuits communication failure never gives children the opportunity to experience the inadequacy of inadequate messages. Suppose that two children are playing a Level II Lotto Game with materials showing one dog, one cat, two dogs, and two cats. One child is the speaker, the other the listener. The speaker says to the listener: "One." Obviously, this utterance is ambiguous. The listener has no way of knowing whether the speaker means one cat or one dog. The practitioner short-circuits communication failure in this situation if he or she immediately prevents the children from experiencing the ambiguity. Typically, the practitioner immediately says: "One cat." When the practitioner does this, he or she deprives both children of learning opportunities. The speaker does not experience the listener's dissatisfaction with the ambiguity; the listener has no need to indicate any displeasure with the message. The speaker does not experience a specific demand for the omitted information; the listener has been given the information the speaker omitted. Furthermore, the listener has no need to request information or to provide feedback. In fact, everyone is content with the speaker's behavior. Everything in the game goes along just fine.

Solutions

The most obvious solution to the problem of chronically short-circuiting communication failure is to force oneself to remain silent when children give inadequate messages. Instead of leaping in, one refrains from saying anything.

One must, however, remain alert to the particular consequences of the communication failure. Does the listener proceed as though the speaker had given an adequate message (e.g, guess whether the speaker means one cat or one dog)? If not, does the listener do anything? One child may complain loudly that he does not know what to do, while another may passively sit until someone else acts. Does the speaker react without any external prompting? Does he spontaneously add the missing information? Do both players seem oblivious to the existence of a problem?

One then intervenes on the basis of this assessment. In doing so, the practitioner has many options. The first is to do as little as possible; this is the preferred option when there is any hope that the children will manage by themselves. The listener's immediate complaint to the speaker is a sign that the communication failure is being handled by the children. The adult remains silent. The second option is to address only the listener: "Does he mean one cat or one dog?". Alternatively, the practitioner may direct the listener to ask the speaker for information: "Ask him, one cat or one dog?". Another option is to address the speaker: "You need to tell him one *what*. One cat? One dog?".

When both children seem bewildered, one's most adaptive option is sometimes to address the children jointly and to include oneself in defining the problem. "We're all mixed up here. Let's start over again."

In any case, the best guideline for selecting an option is the aim of turning communicative functions over to the children: The best option is the one that leaves the largest amount of verbal action to the children. One refrains from doing anything oneself that the children might be expected to do for themselves.

Induction and Rule Violations

The practitioner who is inducted into the child's mode of communication adopts characteristics of the child's communicative behavior that the games are designed to change. The most notable behavioral characteristic of the inducted adult is a tendency to violate the *use words* rule. In Identical

Arrangement Games, for example, the inducted adult reaches over the screen to show the child the correct arrangement of toys. In Lotto, the adult displays pictures while describing them. Instead of using words to make meaning explicit, he or she accompanies visual transmission of information with comments like *This one* and *Do it like this*.

Solution

One origin of this problem is the now-familiar conflict between the traditional role of the teacher and the role the adult plays in communicative work. In traditional teaching, the adult is in an omniscient role and is above the rules. In communicative work, the rules apply to the adult as well as to the children. The *use words* rule means not only that the children must communicate verbally but also that the adult must do so. As the adult, one must enforce this rule so that it applies to oneself as well as to the children, even when it is clear that the children understand pointing better than they understand words.

Diffusing the Focus of Attention

Adequate messages in complex communication games tell listeners which objects are relevant and what to do with those objects. Practitioners who diffuse the focus of attention presuppose the child's ability to infer the relevant objects from statements about the required action. This presupposition is often unwarranted.

For example, suppose that an adult and a child are playing an Identical Arrangement Game and that each player has six toys. The adult as speaker selects only two of the toys and decides not to use the others in this round. He or she then issues a directive about the two toys (e.g., *The man is in the red car.*). It is perfectly reasonable to assume that any adult listener need not be told to select the man, to select the red car, and then to put the man in the car. The adult listener would obviously not need to be told to ignore the woman doll, to ignore the blue car, and so forth. Special-needs children, however, may have difficulty processing all of the information contained in the single statement that would adequately inform an adult. To pack too much information, including presupposed information, into one statement may diffuse the focus of attention.

Solutions

One solution to this problem is to limit the materials so that only a few possible foci exist. The adult might select fewer toys than in the example above. Several specific linguistic tactics may also be useful: building up, breaking down, and ruling out alternatives. To build up a message is to communicate separate bits of information first, then tie them together into a single message (e.g., *The boy. And the truck. Put the boy in the truck.*). Breaking down means conveying the separate pieces of information in one message first, then in separate units (e.g., *Put the green dinosaur under the big tree. The dinosaur. The green one. Put it under the tree. Under the big tree.*). Ruling out alternatives is self-explanatory: *not the red truck, the blue one* or *the green dinosaur, not the black dinosaur.*

Boring Pace

Cultures and individuals differ widely in their preferences for the pace of a game. The English game of cricket seems almost unbearably slow to the American accustomed to the rapid action of baseball. Since adults and children show individual differences in their preferences, there is no fixed rule about how quickly or slowly a game should proceed except that the pace must be fast enough to sustain the child's attention. Children like action. In work with highly distractible children, teachers often aim at slowing the child down, lengthening the child's attention span, and otherwise helping the child to focus on things long enough to learn something about them.

Solutions

Capturing the child's fleeting attention does not, however, necessarily entail slowing the pace of work. A more demanding (sometimes exhausting) alternative is to try to maintain the rules and structure of the game while adapting oneself to the child's rapid pace. If a child needs to be in nearly constant motion, one may try to provide a constant stream of appropriate activities to absorb his or her energy. Each turn is rather brief. Roles are reversed back and forth very quickly. An advantage of assuming a child's rapid pace is the dramatic contrast revealed between effective and ineffective communication. When messages are adequate, the rapid pace proceeds smoothly — the child is engaged, the adult is busy, and things hop along as the child likes them to. When a miscommunication occurs, however, the adult has the opportunity to highlight it. (*Oh-oh. We have to stop. Something's wrong. What happened?*) The sudden plunge into a period of careful deliberation may be more effective in drawing the child's attention to relevant material than would be the case if an entire game were played at a slow pace foreign to the child.

Speeding up the pace is sometimes useful in work with lethargic, passive children. These children seem to need some injection of liveliness. A rapid pace may create a sense that one expects the child to get up and do things, to show some feeling, to move, to react. A rapid pace sometimes captures the attention of the child who seems half asleep most of the time.

Understimulating Content

One sign that a practitioner is using understimulating materials is the practitioner's assertion that attractive toys, lively activities, and other enjoyable aspects of games are overstimulating. It is, of course, perfectly true that some toys and some games are overstimulating to some children. The child with unruly behavior who cannot be trusted to remain within the room is sometimes overstimulated by a game in which he is permitted to jump up and down without having an adult hovering nearby. Often, however, a perception that a game is overstimulating reflects more about the teacher than about the child or the game.

A game may be understimulating in the sense that it is designed to teach something that the child already knows. Practitioners sometimes equate readiness for a game with mastery of its linguistic content. "Easy" games are not always inappropriate. A child may gain a sense of himself as a competent speaker when playing an easy game with a less competent child. A very silent child may benefit from repeated opportunities to say anything, regardless of whether the talking involves any new vocabulary or syntax. A child should not, however, be expected to play games in which he or she is doing nothing new and nothing beneficial.

The fear of overstimulating children with exciting materials and the fear of using challenging content both seem to originate in an outdated image of what teaching, particularly teaching language to young children, is all about. If one's ideal image of learning is a classroom in which silence is broken only by the teacher's questions and the children's correct answers, then fun and the experience of trying before succeeding have no place. In contrast, if one's ideal image of learning language is playful interaction, then laughter, action, and imperfection are perfectly appropriate. A major advantage of games is that the consequences of error are not serious. A burst of laughter may show that the players are enjoying themselves while talking. For children with serious language disabilities, that enjoyment cannot be taken for granted.

In short, the fear of overstimulating children by providing enjoyable materials and demanding linguistic content is considerably more frequent than is actual overstimulation. Furthermore, this fear is considerably more common than the fear of boring the children. Overstimulated children do not learn, but neither do bored children. Unhappily, one sees many more children bored by language lessons than children overstimulated by them.

Flat Tone

The most difficult form of understimulation to describe or change is a practitioner's flat or dull tone. In playing the games, the ideal adult player is modeled on the ideal parent — warm, expressive, affectionate, and respectful of the children's dignity and individuality. The effective adult wants the children to talk and exudes delight at their progress. No particular style of interacting with children seems to single out the effective practitioner; in particular, blatantly emotive people are not necessarily more effective than low-key people. Effective practitioners, however, are never flat or dull in tone, nor are they humorless.

One origin of flatness of tone in playing the games is confusion about what is and is not acceptable behavior for a teacher. The practitioner who seems affectively flat may, in fact, simply need permission to be otherwise. Another source of flatness or dullness is a lack of confidence; the teacher who is preoccupied with the question of whether he or she is playing the game correctly cannot relax and communicate a sense of fun.

Solutions

The extent to which a practitioner may engage in lively play with children, transform the language lesson into an easygoing play period, or otherwise liven up game sessions is sometimes limited by the constraints of the work setting. The speech and language pathologist may be assigned a working space far too small to permit any active games like Picture Positions; the room may be filled up by a big work table and paraphernalia appropriate for desk work with older children and adults. Furthermore, supervisors trained traditionally may be uncomfortable with a feeling of informality and playfulness. One's own training may create a lurking sense that one is not doing what one is supposed to do.

Whether the impediment to livening things up is internal or external, one's best move is to focus attention on the children's needs rather than on the impediments. If the children are bored, they are not learning anything, and one has an obligation to do things differently.

In dealing with traditionally trained colleagues, one may need to be tactful in managing one's work. Liveliness need not be disruptive, and it certainly need not be chaotic. Furthermore, one need not force oneself into ways of working that feel uncomfortable. The practitioner who feels comfortable playing games at a table need not force himself or herself to endure the discomforts of playing on the floor; it is, after all, easy to feel and act lively when one is comfortable.

Conclusions: Beyond Games

The hope of any language intervention program is to have an impact that goes beyond the language intervention setting. Indeed, the problem of generalization from the clinical to the everyday setting dominates current literature on language intervention. Generalization applies to what adult practitioners learn as well as to what children learn. Adult behaviors that are problematic in language intervention sessions are problematic in everyday settings as well. More positively, strategies for creating real demands for communication and for facilitating the child's active participation in verbal communication are not limited to structured games. Avoiding arbitrary demands and rewards while providing meaningful demands and rewards can characterize practitioners' everyday behavior just as it does their game-playing behavior. The games may help practitioners as well as children make their everyday behavior more communicative.

Structuring everyday classroom situations to maximize their communicative potential is an active and difficult process. It is easier to do things for children than to teach them to do those things themselves, and it certainly requires less patience. Just as it is infinitely easier to read children *Little Red Riding Hood* than to help them enact the story as a play, it is easier to serve snack than to help children do so, easier to remain an actor in a starring role than to become a producer-director.

Summary

The transition from a traditional to a communicative approach involves changes in teaching priorities, methods, and the image of the learning situation one wants to create. Problems that characterize and impede that transition include making arbitrary demands for language, monopolizing the speaker role or another central role, short-circuiting communication failure, induction and rule violations, diffusing the focus of attention, setting a boring pace, and providing understimulating content. The structure of the games and tactics useful to adults in playing the games provide some solutions to these problems. The problems practitioners experience while playing the games are problems they experience in everyday settings of interaction with young children as well. Clinicians as well as children need to generalize from the structured clinical setting to the unstructured everyday setting.

References

Allen, K. E. The language impaired child in the preschool: The role of the teacher. *The Directive Teacher*, 1980, *2*(3), 6-10.

Austin, J. L. *How to do things with words*. Oxford: Oxford University Press, 1962.

Bloom, L. *Language development: Form and function in emerging grammars*. Cambridge: MIT Press, 1970.

Bloom, L. Semantic features in language development. In R. Schiefelbusch (Ed.), *Language of the mentally retarded*. Baltimore: University Park Press, 1972.

Bloom, L. *One word at a time*. The Hague: Mouton, 1973.

Brown, R. *A first language: The early stages*. Cambridge: Harvard University Press, 1973.

Brown, R., & Hanlon, C. Derivational complexity and order of acquisition in child speech. In J. R. Hayes (Ed.), *Cognition and the development of language*. New York: Wiley, 1970.

Cazden, C. B. *Child language and education*. New York: Holt, Rinehart and Winston, 1972.

Cook-Gumperz, J. Communicating with young children in the home. *Theory into Practice*, 1979, *18*, 207-212.

Dunn, L. *Peabody picture vocabulary test*. Circle Pines, Minnesota: American Guidance Service, 1965.

Feldman, C. F. Pragmatic features of natural language. *Chicago Linguistic Society Papers*, 1974, 151-160.

Grice, H. P. Logic and conversation. In P. Cole & J. Morgan (Eds.), *Syntax and semantics (Vol. 3)*. New York: Academic Press, 1975.

Hart, B., & Risley, T. Incidental teaching of language in the preschool. *Journal of Applied Behavior Analysis*, 1975, *8*, 411-420.

Muma, J. R., & Pierce, S. Language intervention: Data or evidence? *Topics in Learning and Disabilities*, 1981, *1*(2), 1-11.

Persson, G. *Repetition in English*. Uppsala: Acta Universitatis Upsaliensis, 1974.

Rieke, J., Lynch, L., & Soltman, S. *Teaching strategies for language development*. New York: Grune & Stratton, 1977.

Seibert, J. M., & Oller, D. K. Linguistic pragmatics and language intervention strategies. *Journal of Autism and Developmental Disorders*, 1981, *11*, 75-88.

Weiner, F. F., & Ostrowski, A. A. Effects of listener uncertainty on articulatory inconsistency. *Journal of Speech and Hearing Disorders*, 1979, *44*, 487-493.

Wittgenstein, L. *On certainty*. Oxford: Basil Blackwell, 1969.

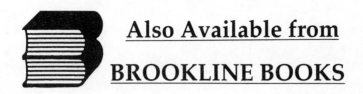

Also Available from
BROOKLINE BOOKS

LANGUAGE DEVELOPMENT IN THE SCHOOL YEARS
By Kevin Durkin

This text will assist any teacher, researcher, or language therapist in better understanding the intricacies of language acquisition, and in interpreting the wealth of information that is available. . . . deals primarily with the important activities of the elementary school years. Syntax, semantics, and phonology are all given their due, but so is the inter-relationship of cognitive development with social-cognitive changes. The application of linguistics and psychology in the school setting to enhance the language process is also broached, which may have an impact for many special educators. — *Rehabilitation Literature*

ISBN 0-914797-27-1   **hardcover**   **$29.95**
20% Discount for Textbook Adoption (6+ copies)

PARENTS AS EDUCATORS
Training Parents to Teach Their Children
By Keith J. Topping

Parents as Educators comprehensively reviews and critiques the effectiveness of programs which train parents to educate their children. It considers a wide range of programs, including those geared toward children with low-income backgrounds, varying ethnic backgrounds, or handicapping conditions. Included are hints for planning projects, a resource directory, and extensive references.

ISBN 0-914797-29-8   **hardcover**   **$29.95**
0-914797-30-1   **softcover**   **$17.95**

WORKING WITH PARENTS
A Practical Guide for Teachers and Therapists
By Roy McConkey, PhD

Aimed at professionals, this draws together for the first time the many procedures for developing successful partnerships with parents. McConkey begins with the premise that cooperation between parents and professionals in a child's education benefits that child and enhances parental participation.

Above all, this is a practical book. There is very little of theory (or professional jargon). There are literally hundreds of detailed suggestions for working with parents, including excellent ideas for individual and group work and special sections relating to fathers, single parents, immigrants, and low-income families. — *American Journal of Mental Deficiency*

ISBN 0-914797-13-1   **hardcover**   **$27.95**
0-914797-14-X   **softcover**   **$17.95**

* BROOKLINE BOOKS * PO Box 1046 * Cambridge MA 02238 * (617)868-0360 *